A celebration of
CUSTOMS & RITUALS
of the world

ROBERT INGPEN & PHILIP WILKINSON

DRAGON'S WORLD

Acknowledgements

Throughout the production of this book the researcher, writer and illustrator have drawn extensively on data gathered by the host of anthropologists working in the field. In particular, the photographs and accounts of those working under the auspices of the National Geographical Society, and published in their magazine, have proved an inspiration.

Dragon's World Ltd
Limpsfield
Surrey RH8 0DY
Great Britain

First published by Dragon's World Ltd 1994

The catalogue record for this book is available from the British Library

ISBN 1 85028 246 3

Editor: Cathy Meeus
Editorial Director: Pippa Rubinstein
Art Director: Robert Ingpen
Designer: Mel Raymond
Jacket design: John Strange
Research: Sally Merriman

Printed in Spain

CONTENTS

A celebration of
CUSTOMS & RITUALS
of the world

FOREWORD

A Celebration of Customs and Rituals of the World is a book that reaches deep into our roots; to what we start learning in the cradle and inherit from preceding generations. This cultural heritage also forms part of what we pass on to generations to come. Through this medium we are guided from birth to death, through all stages of life, each marked with its own special ceremony, somehow assisting us in happiness and sorrow, at work and in our private life.

Customs and rituals are a keystone of human culture. We first get to know them in the family – the main institution for protecting human values, cultural identity and historical continuity. But not all cultural practices are looked upon in positive terms. Whereas some consider customs as *the universal sovereign*, others view them as *the antiquity of error*. It might be so, because customs reflect practices as they have been: and the pace of cultural change and adaptation is sometimes rather slow. Consequently some of them lag behind new standards of behaviour, particularly those approved by the international community in such areas as equal rights between men and women, sharing parental and household responsibilities or the rights of the child. In order to make such customs and rituals conform to changing principles of acceptable international conduct, one has to understand them well and not oversimplify their implications.

Culture may be described as our 'social heritage', the totality of habits and skills that people learn from each other, to a great extent within the family setting. In other words: culture is our entire way of life in a society. In order to appreciate fully how we interact with other people, and also how States interact on the world stage, we need to cultivate a better understanding of the relationship between culture, society and the shaping of individuals.

Customs and rituals seem created to fulfil some of our most basic needs, providing guidance, stability and continuity in our daily lives while giving support in difficult times. Throughout history, humanity has searched for and adopted means of passing on important knowledge to the coming generations. Religion has always been such a tool and many customs and rituals have originated from religious rites. This is why customs and rituals are often imbued with a strong sense of the spiritual and connect us with an order of concepts that gives a higher meaning to our life and our passage through it. Rituals also assist us in creating feelings of fellowship, friendship and kinship between family members, and between individuals, families and societies.

A Celebration of Customs and Rituals of the World is, therefore, both a record of cultural and religious diversity in what is the tradition of human unity, and a plea for tolerance. For, indeed, despite a world of difference, the similarities between cultures are as striking as their differences. Tradition reflects the variety of philosophies and life styles present in families and societies. Learning the customs and rituals of our culture is not an end in itself. They are a link with our past and our future. They help us to understand our own identity. Knowing the customs and traditions of other cultures makes us more tolerant of, and open to, the outside world. In the language of the United Nations, tolerance – the recognition and appreciation of others, the ability to live together with and to listen to others – is the sound foundation of any civil society and the platform on which we try to build world peace.

As the main conduit of culture, the family has a great responsibility in educating individuals and shaping societies. Happy families are an enormous asset. Wrongdoing in families, however, may leave scars with all its members for the rest of their lives. The General Assembly of the United Nations proclaimed 1994 the International Year of the Family. This was in response to the great need for support of families, to empower them in the performance of their vitally important functions. Like the customs and rituals in this book, families come in many different forms and face many different problems; but above all, they have a lot in common.

The entire history of relations within families, societies and among States shows that many evils haunting the world today can be attributed to ignorance with all its adverse ramifications. Ignorance is at the root of too many individuals, groups and nations having perceptions of one another that amount to little more than uninformed stereotypes. This is a dangerous phenomenon, for it breeds prejudice; prejudice engenders mistrust; mistrust develops intolerance; intolerance turns into hatred and hatred provokes wars. By reading an excellent book like *A Celebration of Customs and Rituals of the World*, we may all take one step in the right direction: towards becoming less ignorant about, and more tolerant towards, other people. 1995 was proclaimed the United Nations Year for Tolerance to assist and draw attention to this important process. Ultimately, we will have to learn how to create unity out of the sparkling diversity of cultures that so well epitomize the richness of our human experience.

Henryk J. Sokalski
United Nations Coordinator
for the International Year of the Family

INTRODUCTION

All over the world, at the key points in our lives and the highlights of our calendar, we perform special, ceremonial actions that follow patterns which find parallels in virtually all societies. The form of each of these rituals is prescribed by society, and an official such as a priest is often present to see that the correct formula is followed. The resulting ceremonies are some of the most intriguing human activities.

Sometimes the fascination of the ritual is increased by the addition of less formalized, traditional practices that are not central to the ceremony but are important nonetheless: a

special dance for the bride's unmarried relatives at a wedding; leaving the door open when we go to a funeral. These informal but often ancient customs are the special concern of this book.

From the joy of a child's naming ceremony to the solemnity of our last rites, rituals are constantly being enacted and re-enacted through the cycle of the seasons and of human life. We perform them at harvest time and when we are ill. They help us to resolve disputes with each other and to make contact with our gods. Ceremonies like these are among the most colourful and dramatic of events. Anyone who has witnessed the swirling lion dances of Chinese New Year, or the vast assemblies of people that take place at events like the North African Berber festival of brides, or the potent combination of incense, Gregorian chant and processions during a service in a Catholic basilica in Italy, knows the power that rituals can wield.

While many rituals are highly theatrical and public events, others are intensely intimate, human experiences that touch us to the core. And in many cases the two aspects co-exist. Coming as they do at life's turning-points, rituals often seem to transform their participants. In many cultures people are said to be 'reborn' during a ritual. Sometimes, as at a birth ceremony, initiation or wedding, a new name may be given. And the transformation can be profound. There is a sense, for example, in which a Jewish boy becomes a man during his Bar Mitzvah. He is still only 13 years old, but he commits himself to key religious and moral obligations and he may from now on be counted among the *minyan* or quorum of men required for prayers. Part of the power of rituals comes from the way they use symbols to convey ideas, emotions and depths of meaning in a way that is impossible through speech alone. The manner in which, for example, a communal meal with special food may evoke meanings of community, sharing, or reconciliation can make such occasions truly moving. It is not surprising, then, that participants in rituals are usually deeply involved in what they are doing: the emotions stirred may be some of the most profound we experience and they may have repercussions that last for the rest of our lives.

UNIVERSAL PRACTICES

Ceremonies and rituals occur in all types of societies. Many similar rituals appear in widely differing cultures – the details may differ widely from place to place, but there are many common elements and the occasions for the rituals are the same. In particular, the turning points of birth, coming of age, marriage and death are marked with their own special rituals. Most societies also follow special rituals relating to the processes of basic human survival – food production, eating and drinking, and healing the sick – and ceremonies connected with the organization of social groups – initiations for new group members, rituals to help resolve disputes between individuals or groups. Finally, there are also the rituals that look beyond the mundane, to the worlds of spirituality, religion and art. Many of these ceremonies are performed as the need arises, but some are linked closely to particular days – the myriad of calendar customs and festivities that punctuate the year in societies all over the world.

Ceremonies and rituals fulfil certain basic human needs. Because most rituals are collective, they often foster cooperation and collaboration, and help to cement the ties that join individuals and communities together. On a big national occasion like a carnival or a coronation, thousands of people may come together in a communal celebration. But even the more intimate, family ceremonies can demand that everyone works together and plays their part. Rituals, from the naming of a child to great state occasions, can help to unify families and whole societies. So important is the correct conduct of the ceremony, indeed, that in certain cultures a subsequent misfortune is often blamed on the fact that a ritual has been performed incorrectly.

Another human aspiration that rituals fulfil is the need to transcend everyday life. Ceremonies are frequently occasions upon which the emotions of the participants are lifted beyond their normal range. Singing, dancing, drumming, special costumes and masks, heightened or poetic language, the use of incense or fire, and colourful processions – all these things can create a sense of elevation onto another plane of existence for the participant, and sometimes for the spectators too.

Finally, through the widespread connection with religion, ceremonies and rituals help to provide a sense of order in what can often seem a chaotic world. The repetition of actions and words in ceremonies that have been followed sometimes for hundreds of years can create a feeling of coherence and continuity that provides a sense of our place in the larger universe.

Continuity

Not surprisingly, rituals have been performed since the earliest days of our development. The careful burials of our Neandertal predecessors, the corpses carefully arranged with offerings around them, may be evidence of the first funerals. The cave paintings of Lascaux and Niaux have suggested to some authorities magic ceremonies before the hunt or ancient fertility rites. The Abbé Henri Breuil (1877-1961), expert on Palaeolithic art, said that ancient paintings of human figures dressed up as animals 'evoke the dancing and initiation ceremonies of living peoples or represent the sorcerers or gods of the Upper Palaeolithic'.

Most human ceremonies have a long history. Key elements in rituals, such as the burial or cremation of a body or the dance or feast that forms the climax of a wedding have been used for millennia. The very words of some ceremonies have survived unchanged for centuries. In some cases this is because they have the sanction of a powerful or charismatic religion. Christians and Muslims, for example, still use formulas for prayer that were laid down by Christ and Muhammad. In addition, there is the sense of awe that people may feel when they take part in a ceremony that has been conducted in the same way, perhaps in the same place or on the same day in the year, for generations.

The special power of ancient and oft-repeated words and actions enhances many ceremonies and, some would say, makes them all the more ceremonious. When the Duke of Norfolk, as Britain's Earl Marshal, was organizing the coronation of Queen Elizabeth II in 1953, he was asked whether he wanted the sevices of a theatrical director, so that he could exploit the full impact of the ceremony. He turned down the idea, realizing that the ritual has its own theatricality, which emerges naturally from the order of the events themselves, which have evolved over hundreds of years. The ceremony is impressive, thrilling and moving enough without additional gimmickry.

Living traditions

But the most vibrant rituals are not static, fossilized affairs that never change. They are continually being transformed, with elements being added as cultures change. One of the best examples of how a ritual can be transformed while keeping some of its ancient elements is the celebration of the month of May in Europe. For the pagan Celts, May Day was Beltane, a festival in which fire was used to celebrate the start of summer. They rolled wheels of fire down hillsides, lit bonfires, and drove their cattle through the flames in a ceremony of purification. Meanwhile, the people performed a circular dance alluding to the circling sun. The Romans paid homage to the goddess Flora, who presided over flowers and fruits, at this time of the year. And still earlier peoples worshipped the newly blossoming trees. All these elements come together in the tradition of garlands of flowers and circular dances around the maypole, still practised in some rural areas. But in modern times May Day has been transformed still further, into a holiday associated with socialism. The early Christian church, as it spread through Europe, also appropriated existing rituals, deliberately timing festivals such as Christmas and Ascension Day to coincide with the dates of traditional pagan and Roman rites.

Rituals transform themselves in other ways. People who have been taken over by a foreign power often adopt, or have imposed upon them, elements of the rituals of their new rulers. And the vagaries of fashion have also played their part in moulding the character of many customs by encouraging people to look to other cultures for their ritual inspiration. This tendency is often revealed in the clothes worn by the participants. Thus it is not uncommon for Japanese couples to adopt western dress (dark suit for the man, white bridal gown for the woman) for part of their wedding ceremonies, reverting to traditional Japanese costumes at another stage in the proceedings.

New rituals

Many of the ceremonies that are common to all cultures, especially the rites of passage, are couched in religious terms, are presided over by a religious leader and may require some form of religious oath on the part of the participants. In a modern secular society, such ceremonies leave some people feeling uncomfortable. Yet many non-religious people still feel the need for ritual to mark important events in their lives. So some people in the West have begun to devise alternative ceremonies, rituals that fulfil the needs of the

rites of passage, without the religious element. In so doing they have shown another way in which rituals can evolve.

Welfare State International, a company that specializes in theatrical productions and large-scale theatrical events – performances that often involve everything from fireworks to food and politics to puppets – has also helped to devise and perform a number of naming ceremonies for newborn children around the world. In locations as diverse as a hilltop in the North York moors in England and a courtyard in Baltimore, they have created moving and dramatic ceremonies involving elements such as the release of doves, specially written songs and a personal Book of Naming for each child, recording the event and the names of other children named on the same day.

Other organizations, such as the British Humanist Association, have produced outlines for funeral ceremonies for people who would not have wished for a religious funeral. A structure has been devised, with recommendations for each stage in the ritual, from opening remarks, words to speak about life and death in general, a specific tribute to the deceased, and the committal itself.

In their different ways these two types of alternative ritual demonstrate how a sensitive and thoughtful approach can create ceremonies that are appropriate for people from a wide range of social and philosophical backgrounds. They show how, even in a secular society, rituals can continue to occupy a vital place – at the centre of our lives.

CALENDAR
OF
CUSTOMS

Throughout the world, the calendar is punctuated by regular festivals. From the winter festivals like Christmas and Diwali, when the night sky glitters with candles and coloured lights, to the rituals of springtime and the summer solstice, these are times of celebration that can provide enjoyment on a national and even international scale.

At these times of the year entire populations can take to the streets. The processions and revellers of the world's great carnivals; Europeans celebrating May morning or midsummer and getting up to greet the dawn; the crowds who line the streets for Holy Week processions in Spain and Italy; the hundreds of ordinary people who turn out when a ruler appears before the people; the thousands who gather for firework displays on Guy Fawkes' night in England or Independence Day in the USA – all are taking part in festivities that, for a while at least, unite people in ways that are impossible at other times.

Often this happens because the celebrations are highly enjoyable and entertaining in their own right. Perhaps this is what makes ceremonies like May Day dancing so compulsive. We may no longer look to the gods to ensure the fertility of the soil, but the rituals of May Day, with their maypoles and flowers, Morris dancers and people dressed in green branches, still attract support, perhaps because they offer a welcome change from the mundane everyday routines.

The variety of celebrations

Calendar customs have amazing variety, but there are a handful of reasons behind them. Some are religious: they mark the birth of a deity or religious leader, the anniversary of a key event in the history of the religion. Others are agricultural, relating to the calendar of tilling, planting and harvesting. Still others are local or national festivals, commemorating the birth or death of a hero or an important national event such as the anniversary of the founding of the state. And some calendar customs seem simply to mark the passing of time itself – midsummer or midwinter, the coming of the sun or the end of the rains.

Frequently a calendar custom seems to be held for a combination of these reasons. A festival of the sun may also have religious overtones; a modern political celebration may take place on a date previously set aside for a traditional agricultural festival.

Seasonal festivities

Probably the most ancient of the calendar customs relate to the passing of the seasons. All over the world there are festivals of winter and summer. These may focus on a change in the weather, a date in the calendar like New Year, or on the actual solstices, the shortest and longest days of the year.

Many of these festivals no doubt derive from an ancient question: how can we predict the seasons? The answer lay in the movements of the heavenly bodies, and the number of ancient stone alignments and circles that are lined up with the positions of the sun and stars is testimony to this. Especially popular, as at Stonehenge and elsewhere, were alignments with the point on the horizon at which the sun rose at midsummer. Midsummer is still a widely celebrated seasonal festival, whether linked to a holy day such as the feast of St John the Baptist, as it is in many Christian countries, or celebrated in its own right, as in places where traditional religions prevail.

The other seasons also bring their celebrations. Winter festivals, linked in many places with New Year or with religious days like Christmas, are widespread. So are celebrations of spring and autumn, frequently connected with events in the agricultural or natural calendars. In Florence, for example, spring is celebrated on Ascension Day, the fortieth day after Easter, with the cricket festival. All over the city, stalls sell cages each containing a singing cricket: the creature's song is held to be a sign that spring has arrived. People buy a cricket and take it to the Cascine Park, where there are picnics and games. It is a good omen for the remainder of the year if the cricket is still singing when it is time for the children to go to bed.

RELIGIOUS FESTIVALS

If some of the traditional calendar celebrations seem remote, many provide a vital focus for the lives of millions of people. This is true with many of the religious festivals. Jews and Muslims, Christians and Hindus, Buddhists and Sikhs – all structure their year around calendar festivals. The highlights of the religious year (Christmas or Easter for Christians, Diwali or Holi for Hindus, for example) are marked by calendar festivals that play a vital part in the lives of the faithful.

But even these ancient religious festivals change their focus through time. Christmas, for example, is celebrated by many who hardly consider themselves Christians. Such people give presents and send cards, eat festive food, and even put up Christmas trees in their homes. The fact that they are doing this suggests that they are responding to values that are close to the Christian religion, such as the importance of friends and family. But it may also show that Christmas and earlier pre-Christian midwinter festivals fulfil a fundamental need to find a way of brightening the darkness of the bleak northern midwinter. This process is typical of the way in which festivals can change some of their meaning and purpose while the time of year at which they are celebrated remains unchanged.

THE AGRICULTURAL CALENDAR

Many calendar festivals can be traced back to roots in the agricultural year. Frequently these were connected with harvest and sometimes with the planting of the crops (see Hunting and harvesting, pages 116-24). But festivities

MAJOR INTERNATIONAL FESTIVALS

BUDDHIST

Because the Buddhist calendar and days of celebration vary from place to place and between the different branches of Buddhism, festivals to mark key events in the life of the Lord Buddha such as his birth, his enlightenment, first sermon, and death, are observed on different days in different countries.

could be held much earlier in the season, with the preparation of the ground. This is the case with the English traditional celebration of Plough Monday, when farm work begins in earnest again after Christmas with ploughing. A church service is sometimes held on the Sunday after Twelfth Night, at which all the agricultural work of the coming year is prayed for and blessed. On the day after, there is sometimes a procession through the streets, in which young men dressed in tatters haul an old-fashioned plough and demand money from the people they meet. It used to be the tradition for them to plough up the gardens of those who refused to pay.

Other milestones of the agricultural calendar were also attended with festivities. May Day, for example, was widely celebrated in Europe as the time when flocks and herds were turned on to their summer grazing land. Dancing around maypoles, the crowning of a young woman as May Queen, and making garlands of may (hawthorn) were also common in England.

NATIONAL DAYS

Nearly every country has at least one day on which the nation itself is celebrated. It might be an independence day, the date of the founding of a republic, or some other key date in the history of the state. In the USA, for example, American Independence Day, the anniversary of the day on which the republic was first declared, is celebrated on 4 July. In France there is Bastille Day on 14 July, the anniversary of the storming of the royal prison during the revolution. The Swedes have Flag Day on 6 June, the day on which Gustavus Vasa became the first king of an independent Sweden. The Australians have Anniversary Day on 26 January, celebrating the landing of Captain James Cook in Botany Bay in 1770. Most of the 'young' African nations have independence days, which form important focuses of national identity. In addition, there are workers' celebrations of socialism and trade unionism – usually called Labour Days, often on 1 May, but sometimes on other dates.

CHINESE

January/February	New Year
February/March	Lantern Festival
March/April	Festival of Pure Brightness
May/June	Dragon Boat Festival
August	All Souls'
September/October	Double Ninth Festival
November/December	Winter Solstice

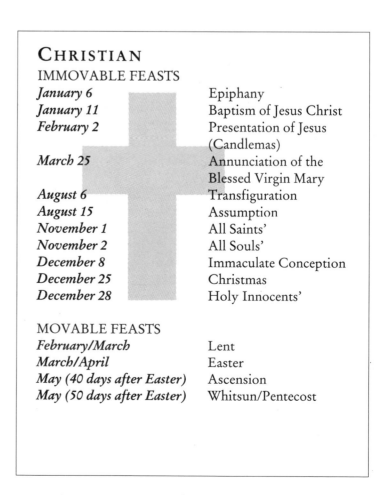

CHRISTIAN

IMMOVABLE FEASTS

January 6	Epiphany
January 11	Baptism of Jesus Christ
February 2	Presentation of Jesus (Candlemas)
March 25	Annunciation of the Blessed Virgin Mary
August 6	Transfiguration
August 15	Assumption
November 1	All Saints'
November 2	All Souls'
December 8	Immaculate Conception
December 25	Christmas
December 28	Holy Innocents'

MOVABLE FEASTS

February/March	Lent
March/April	Easter
May (40 days after Easter)	Ascension
May (50 days after Easter)	Whitsun/Pentecost

Sometimes, the national focus is on a saint or mythological hero who has come to symbolize the country. Thus in England St George's Day is marked on 23 April by flying the English flag, while the Welsh celebrate St David's Day on 1 March, when it is traditional to wear a leek or a daffodil, and the Irish wear shamrocks on St Patrick's Day (17 March). In other places, more recent heros are commemorated: people in the Central African Republic, for example, remember the death of President Boganda on 29 March. And then there are the ubiquitous holidays for the birthday of the monarch, celebrated from Britain to Bhutan.

Other national commemorations centre on events in military history. Amongst these are the exceptions to the rule that calendar customs are times of celebration and joy, since they include the days on which people all over the world remember those who have died for their countries. Armistice Day (11 November), with the laying of wreaths to remember those who lost their lives in battle, is widely kept.

But it is not the only remembrance day. In Australia, for example, Anzac Day (25 April) marks the anniversary of the first Gallipoli landings in 1915.

A WORLD OF CALENDARS

The pages that follow describe a selection of the calendar festivals that occur all over the world. They are arranged, for the convenience of the majority of readers, by the widely used western months, and movable feasts are allotted to the month during which they often occur, although in some years they will occur in different months. But different calendars are used in different cultures and by the adherents of different religions.

The usual western calendar is called the Gregorian calendar, after Pope Gregory, who introduced it in 1582. It is a solar calendar with months of lengths varying from 28 to 31 days; an extra day is added every fourth (leap) year. The Hindu calendar is a lunar calendar of 12 months, each of 29 days and 12 hours, with

HINDU

Chaitra S9	Ramanavami (Birthday of Lord Rama)
Sravana S11-15	Jhulanayatra ('Swinging the Lord Krishna')
Sravana S15	Rakshabandhana ('Tying on the Lucky Threads')
Bhadrapada K8	Janamashtami (Birthday of Lord Krishna)
Asvina S1-10	Dusshera (Durga-puja)
Asvina K15	Diwali (Lakshmi-puja)
Kartikka S15	Guru Nanak Jananti (Birthday of Guru Nanak)
Magha K13	Mahasivaratri (Great Night of Lord Siva)
Phalguna S14	Holi

ISLAMIC

1 Muharram	New Year
12 Rabi 1	Birthday of Muhammad
27 Rajab	Night of Ascent of Muhammad to Heaven
1 Ramadan	Beginning of month of fasting
27 Ramadan	'Night of Power'
1 Shawwal	Eid-ul-Fitr (marking end of Ramadan)
8-13 Dhu-I-Hijja	Annual pilgrimage ceremonies at Mecca
10 Dhu-I-Hijja	Eid-ul-Adha (Feast of the Sacrifice)

occasional extra months added to reconcile the difference between this lunar year and the solar year of 365 days. The Jews use a system with alternating 29-day and 30-day months, again with the occasional addition of an extra month. Muslims have a 354-day year, also using alternating 30- and 29-day months, with the intercalation of one day at the end of the 12th month at stated intervals. This short year means that the western month in which a given Muslim festival occurs gradually rotates through a 30-year cycle. For this reason, it is not helpful to allocate Muslim festivals to specific western months. These festivals have therefore been generally omitted from the month-by-month survey of calendar festivals that follows, although the annual pilgrimage to Mecca and the Feast of the Sacrifice are included in the illustration for July to represent the Islamic world. In China an official Civilian Calendar based on the western Gregorian calendar is used, although the traditional Chinese calendar is used in other parts of the Chinese world, such as Tibet, Hong Kong, Singapore and Malaysia. The months of the Japanese calendar are basically the same as those of the Gregorian calendar.

A range of calendars is used in traditional societies, even where central governments have adopted one of the international calendars. Lunar calendars are common in such societies, and the months may be named after prominent stages in the agricultural cycle or after the prevalent hunting quarry. Thus a traditional Papua New Guinea calendar names the months after fish that may be caught: there are months called Mumbe'eng (Blue-speckled Parrotfish Moon), Momo'eng (Tiger Shark Moon), and Mupi'eng (Flying Fish Moon). But whatever the calendar, the festivals can cross boundaries of geography and religion. Chinese businessmen in the West, who acknowledge the western calendar, still celebrate the traditional New Year. South American Catholics go on pilgrimages to places where the Incas worshipped the Sun. Such festivities demonstrate the power of customs and rituals to bring us triumphantly together.

JEWISH

1-2 Tishri	Rosh Hashana (New Year)
10 Tishri	Yom Kippur (Day of Atonement)
15-21 Tishri	Sukkot (Feast of Tabernacles)
23 Tishri	Simchat Torah (Rejoicing of the Law)
25 Kislev - 2-3 Tevet	Chanukah (Feast of Dedication)
14-15 Adar	Purim (Feast of Lots)
15-22 Nisan	Pesach (Passover)
6-7 Sivan	Shavuoth (Festival of Weeks)

JAPANESE

1-3 January	Oshogatsu (New Year)
3 March	Ohinamatsuri (Girl's Festival)
5 May	Kodomo no Hi (Boy's Festival)
7 July	Hoshi matsuri (Star Festival)
End of July	Obon (All Souls')

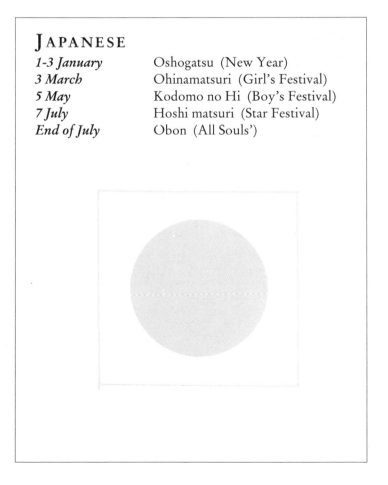

NEW YEARS
Southern Italians throw pots out of windows. People gather around bonfires in northern Europe. The Chinese perform lion and dragon dances to welcome their new year (each year is named for one of 12 animals). In the Christian world, the gifts of the Magi to the infant Christ are remembered. In Scotland the haggis is ceremonially piped in. In many places the new year is announced with music and lanterns in the streets.

January

New Year is a time of celebration, of looking forward to new beginnings and challenges. In the West, many people stay up, keeping a vigil as the old year dies. As the clock strikes midnight, toasts are drunk and merrymaking begins in earnest. A joyous beginning, it is hoped, will portend a good year ahead.

Often the first event of the year, or the first person you meet, is held to have a special significance. Hence the British tradition of 'first footing', in which an attractive (usually male and preferably dark-haired) visitor is hoped for immediately after midnight. He will enter bringing a gift, in many areas a piece of coal for the fire.

Bonfires are lit in many places in Europe, to burn the remains of the old year. In China, it was traditional to burn an image of the household god to mark the end of the old year and the beginning of the new. In Italy, windows are traditionally opened to let out the old year. Indeed, in southern Italy it is the custom to hurl old pots, pans and even pieces of furniture out of the open windows on New Year's Eve – a very graphic illustration of the abandonment of the old in favour of the new.

Many places have traditional foods for their New Year celebrations. Pig's trotters with lentils are eaten in Italy. The lentils symbolize coins and are said to bring prosperity in the coming year. In some parts of Scotland red herrings are eaten at Hogmanay. One of the best known Scottish New Year customs is the singing of 'Auld Lang Syne', while everyone links arms together.

Chinese New Year normally occurs in either January or February. It is traditionally heralded with fire crackers, gifts of money and lion or dragon dances. Festivities end with the Lantern Festival, on the first full moon of the year, symbolizing the return of light and looking forward to the coming of spring.

CARNIVAL
In Venice, carnival revellers go masked; elsewhere, from Africa to the Americas, they may dress in anything from feathers to pierrot costumes. Men and women flirt during Holi in India. In the West, lovers send each other Valentine cards on 14 February. In England pancakes are eaten on Shrove Tuesday, before the start of Lent on Ash Wednesday.

February

In many places, February is the month of carnival. This is a good example of a custom that combines and recombines religious and secular elements. Carnival is a period of celebration and indulgence before fasting. Going without meat at this time of the year was often necessary in the days before modern food preservation. A practical necessity was turned into a religious fast – the Christian period of Lent.

On Shrove Tuesday (or Mardi Gras), in places as far apart as Rio de Janeiro, Venice and New Orleans, people take to the streets in their thousands, with dancing, music, and rich food. In Venice people dress up and wear highly decorated, glittering masks. In Mexico and Brazil there are parades with colourful floats, and everywhere there is dancing through the streets. Ash Wednesday follows Shrove Tuesday, signalling the beginning of Lent. The name Ash Wednesday is a reference to the sackcloth and ashes of the Christian penitent. The day itself marks the beginning of a 40-day period of austerity.

In northern India and Pakistan, the full moon at the end of this month marks the festival of Holi and the beginning of spring. It starts with spring cleaning and bonfires are lit at dusk (on which old belongings are burned). Men and women dance and flirt, squirt pink-dyed water at each other, or throw powder coloured pink, green or saffron.

The feeling of renewal is also expressed in Jewish communities, where Tu B'shvat is celebrated. New trees are planted for every baby born on this day – cypresses for the girls, cedars for the boys. Children in Israel also plant trees at this time.

Chinese Buddhists and Taoists remember the goddess of mercy, Guan Yin, at this time. Gifts are brought to her shrines, and prayers are said for the coming year.

SPRING AND RENEWAL
Throughout Europe there are traditional Easter celebrations. In Switzerland and Germany effigies of winter are burned. The Japanese display dolls for the girls' festival, and the Irish wear shamrocks on St Patrick's Day.

March

The great Christian festival of resurrection, Easter, often falls in March. Traditions such as the giving of eggs (sugar and chocolate confections in western Europe, exquisitely decorated hens' eggs in central and eastern Europe) point to the pre-Christian origins of this festival. Good Friday is a time for abstinence, solemn processions, and passion plays. In Mexico, Easter Saturday is celebrated with firecrackers; Easter Sunday is usually the time for the giving of eggs and feasting.

Processions are common in Holy Week, especially in the Mediterranean, where throngs of cowled figures pass through the streets carrying crosses and religious effigies.

In many places there are special celebrations on the spring equinox on or around 21 March. Masked parades in the Austrian Tirol, throwing effigies of 'Death' or 'Winter' into rivers in Slovakia, burning effigies of 'Winter' in Germany or Switzerland – these are all examples of customs that usher in the spring.

For Hindus, March sees the festival of Ganguar, devoted to Gauri or Parvati, wife of Siva and goddess of fertility and marital happiness. Most Hindus in India also celebrate Ramanavami, commemorating the birthday of Lord Rama. There is fasting and serious religious discussions are held, but there is a more lighthearted aspect to the celebration – the temples are beautifully decorated.

The Chinese, especially those in the fishing communities from Fujian to Hong Kong and Taiwan, celebrate the birthday of Mazu, the goddess of the sea. Shrines are set up on the sea fronts and prayers are said for good weather and good catches.

An important Japanese festival is the girls' festival, Ohinamatsuri, which falls on 3 March. The highlight is a display of dolls and miniature household items, which may have been handed down through the generations.

ALL FOOLS' AND SPRING FEASTS
April is presided over by the figure of Spring and by the
fool, who reigns for the first 12 hours of April 1.
Meanwhile, more solemn festivals, such as Jewish
Passover and the birthday of Buddha, may be celebrated
at this time of the year. In China people sweep the tombs
of their ancestors at the festival of Qing Ming.

April

One of the most widespread customs linked to this month is April Fool's or All Fools' Day, on the first day of the month. On this day tricks and practical jokes are played on people in a custom that is common throughout Europe and Asia. Traditionally the foolery stops at midday, but it may sometimes continue for longer, as in parts of Scotland where the jokes continue until 2 April. Celebrations at this time may have their origins in the fact that this day marks the end of the spring equinox, a point at which night and day are of equal length all over the world.

The Jewish festival of Passover often falls at this time, marking the end of the captivity of the Israelites in Egypt. Houses must be clean and tidy for Passover, and this may be one of the origins of the custom of 'spring cleaning'.

In China, Qing Ming, the tomb-sweeping festival, is held. People visit the shrines and tombs of their ancestors, where they sweep, clear weeds from the ground and repaint the inscriptions. Sacrificial gifts in the form of imitation money and paper clothes may be burned at the tombs.

For Buddhists in Japan, the traditional date of the birthday of the Buddha occurs in this month. Images of the infant Buddha are ceremonially washed with sweet tea.

Thailand used to celebrate New Year in this month, on Songkran Day, 13 April. Nowadays, Thais celebrate New Year on 31 December, but the traditional water festivals of Songkran are still held. Temples and statues of the Buddha are sprinkled with water, but there are also less formal rituals, in which anyone is likely to get drenched. Boat races and water-borne pageants are staged, and a Songkran Princess is appointed, who is carried through the streets on a wooden horse.

Some spring festivals are linked to the harvest. This is true of Baisakhi, an old harvest festival of northern India. This is also a time of celebration for Sikhs, since the founder of their religion, Guru Nanak, began his missionary work on this day.

FERTILITY AND PEACE
In Europe, May sees processions of girls garlanded with flowers dancing around the maypole, and traditional dances such as the English Morris Dance. Jews celebrate the giving of the Ten Commandments at Shavuoth. In Japan, carp-shaped streamers mark the traditional boys' festival.

May

The Romans had a festival of Maia, the mother of the god Mercury, which was celebrated on the first day of her month. This may be the origins of May Day celebrations that are still held widely in Europe. It marked the time when flocks and herds were turned on to their summer grazing. The Celts called this time of year Beltane, and lit fires in celebration.

Dancing around a maypole on May Day is traditional in many parts of Europe, from Wales and England to Provence and Bavaria. The celebrations of May have long been linked with fertility ceremonies. A common feature of European May Day celebrations is often known as Green George. He is a man dressed from head to toe in leafy green branches, another obvious symbol of fruitful nature.

In the 20th century, the May Day festival was taken over in many places by the politicians, as a day on which the virtues of socialism were celebrated. Although the great May Day parades of the former USSR are a thing of the past, the day is still celebrated as Labour Day in many countries.

In the Jewish world, this is the time of Shavuoth, the festival that marks the giving of the Ten Commandments to Moses on Mount Sinai. Flowers and plants are generally used to decorate the synagogue.

Ascension Day is celebrated by Christians on the fortieth day after Easter, followed by Whit Sunday ten days later. This marks the time at which Christ's disciples received the Holy Spirit and began to preach about Jesus. The festival is a popular time for baptisms and, since candidates would dress in white, 'whit' may originally have been 'white'. Jews know this festival as Pentecost.

In Japan, 5 May is a national holiday called Kodomo no Hi, a boys' festival. Streamers made of cloth or paper in the shape of carp are put on top of wooden poles.

THE COMING OF THE SUN
Inca sun festivals are still re-enacted in South America. Dancing around a cross decorated with leaves is the focus of summer festivals in parts of Scandinavia. Midsummer may be greeted with elaborate feathered costumes in Central America. White robed druids welcome the midsummer sun at Stonehenge, and in China the Dragon Boat Festival is celebrated.

June

The summer solstice at the end of June is celebrated in many places around the world, as it has been ever since early people made stone circles or alignments and watched the sun rise over the menhirs on midsummer day. Modern-day Druids still recreate these rituals in a midsummer ceremony at Stonehenge in England.

There are still midsummer fairs in England, festive bonfires in Scandinavia, the Netherlands, Germany, Spain and Portugal, and other celebrations at midsummer in many parts of Europe. In Spain the summer solstice is linked with the feast day of St John, and bonfires are lit on the shortest night of the year, 23 June, especially in coastal areas where the festivities take place on the beach.

The Christian feast of Corpus Christi, a commemoration of Christ's Last Supper with his disciples takes place in June. It is a time of rejoicing, during which consecrated bread is carried through streets decorated with flowers. In some places, such as rural Mexico, the celebration of Corpus Christi has become united with the old pagan sun celebration.

Another combination of pagan and religious feasts is the summer festival in Sweden. A celebration of summer with dancing in national costume, this was originally a pagan feast, but was taken over by the church as the feast of St John the Baptist.

In the Chinese world this is the time of year of the Dragon Boat Festival, Duan Yang. Races between long narrow brightly painted rowing boats are accompanied by the striking of gongs and the waving of flags. The festival is held in memory of the suicide by drowning of the poet Qu Yuan in 279 BC.

June is also a time of merrymaking for some of the peoples of Africa. The Yoruba people of south-western Nigeria, for example, have a festival in honour of the ancestors in early June called Egungun.

PROCESSIONS AND PILGRIMAGES
Muslims may make the pilgrimage to Mecca at this time of the year. This is followed by the festival of Eid-ul-Adha, at which animals are sacrificed. The Japanese decorate graves with flowers during the festival of Obon. In the Hindu festival of Rakshabandhana, girls tie coloured bands around their brothers' wrists. The Sri Lankan feast of Kandy Perahera involves processions with elephants.

July

The Japanese hold a festival to commemorate the spirits of dead ancestors at this time of year. During this festival, called Obon, graves are decorated with flowers, incense is burned and special prayers are said. Reeds of hemp are also burned, and coloured lanterns are set up, to give light to show the spirits the way home. The festival ends with traditional dancing and singing. July also sees the launching of huge fish in the sea at Toyahama. The fish constructed of bamboo frames covered with cloth, are made by local fisherman in honour of the gods of the ocean.

In Sri Lanka there is the celebration of Kandy Perahera, a ten-day Buddhist festival. The highlight is a procession of elephants, musicians and dancers, in which a holy relic, one of Buddha's teeth, is ceremoniously carried through the streets.

This month also sees the beginning of Buddhist time of abstinence. In Thailand, for example, many men enter a monastery for a week or more. Those who do not are still involved – they offer food to the monks.

In the Hindu world, this is the time of Rakshabandhana, or Rakhi. This is a celebration of brotherhood and sisterhood. Girls tie bands of red and gold-coloured cotton or silk around their brothers' wrists, symbolizing the bond between siblings.

July (or August) contains a solemn day in the Jewish calendar: Tish B'av, a day of mourning and fasting commemorating the destruction of the First and Second Temples in Jerusalem (in 586 BC and AD 70 respectively). Tish B'av itself is the final day of nine days of mourning, during which meat is not eaten and weddings are not performed. A black curtain is draped over the Ark in the synagogue, and only a single flickering light illuminates the synagogue. Poems of suffering and the Book of Lamentations are read.

CAESAR'S MONTH
Named for the Emperor Augustus, this month sees traditional dancing at Welsh Eistedfodau. Mexicans celebrate Independence Day with foods that are the same colours as their national flag. In Britain it was traditional to give thanks for the first loaf baked from the year's corn. A Hindu statue reminds us that this is harvest time in India too.

August

August was named in 8 BC for the Roman Emperor Augustus, because many of the key events in his life took place in August. The Italians still celebrate Ferragosto, the festival of the Emperor Augustus. Today the festival takes place on 15 August, which coincides with the Christian feast of the Assumption, the day on which the Virgin Mary ascended to heaven. There is consequently a mixture of sacred and secular in the celebrations. Assumption processions and celebrations are common in many Catholic countries. A similar coming together of religious and secular celebrations occurs in Mexico, where St Augustine's Day (28 August) and national Independence Day (15 September) frame a double festival.

The month of August is a harvest month in many places in the northern hemisphere. In Britain, 1 August used to be known as Lammas, from Anglo-Saxon words meaning 'loaf mass'. This was a festival of the beginning of the harvest, when thanks were given for the loaf baked from the year's first corn. In addition, semi-common lands were thrown open for grazing at this time. In the Celtic world, 1 August was Lughnasa, a feast day in honour of the god Lugh. Irish celebrations and Scottish Lammas fairs probably have their roots in this ancient Celtic feast.

Another August harvest festival is celebrated in India, particularly in the southwest. It is a joyous time, when people decorate their houses with flowers, put on their best clothes, and sit down to a great feast. Food is also distributed to the poor and to the brahmins. There are boat races and fireworks in the evening. This is also the time of Krishna's birthday, Janamashtami.

In Wales, the Eisteddfodau, traditional festivals of the arts, are held during in the summer. The robed bards help to keep the Welsh language and culture alive.

CELEBRATION OF THE HARVEST
Celebrations in the field on the way home, and in the church were traditional at the end of European harvests. The fruits of the fields are still brought to church and the custom of making corn dollies continues. The grape harvest in France and Spain heralds similar festivities. In India there is the festival of the elephant-headed god Ganesh.

September

In the northern hemisphere, this is above all a time of harvest, when the crops are got in and preparations are made for winter. Thanks are given for the crops, and in many places gifts are given to the poor and needy. In England, there used to be triumphant processions through the villages when the harvest was at last completed. In addition, displays of corn, fruit and vegetables were set up in the churches and services of thanksgiving held. Nowadays, harvest processions are less usual, but church services of thanksgiving for the harvest remain common, even in cities. Traditionally, the last of the corn would be twisted into a corn dolly in the shape of a person or a cornucopia. In an interesting parallel, rice dollies are made in Melanesia with the last of the harvest. In wine-producing areas, the grape harvest is a cause for celebration.

In the alpine communities of Switzerland and in Germany, the descent of the shepherds and their flocks from the mountain summer pastures is a cause for special festivities. The animals are decorated with flowers and the people often dress in national costume to welcome them back for another winter.

In China mid-autumn is celebrated at the festival of Zhong Qui, held on the day of, or just before the full moon. Mooncakes are baked in commemoration of a revolt against the Mongols in the 14th century (the signal to revolt was written on papers hidden in the cakes). Lion dances are popular, as are parades of children. People carrying lanterns go to the nearest hill and watch the moon rise.

This is a time of many festivals in India. In Orissa and Maharashtra, for example, there is Ganesh Chaturthi, the festival of Ganesh, the beloved elephant-headed god. Images of Ganesh are set up on street corners and are paraded through the streets on trucks.

FASTING AND FEASTING

Hallowe'en torches and pumpkin lanterns, together with images of beer-drinking from Bavaria, set a tone of licence and revelry. Fireworks and demonic effigies also play a part in the Hindu festival of Dusshera. In China, Chong Yang is a cause for hilltop processions. The Jewish scholar recalls Simchat Torah, the time at which the cycle of readings of the Law is completed.

October

The period of the end of September and beginning of October is the time of many Jewish festivals. The first is Rosh Hashana, the Jewish New Year, followed by Yom Kippur, the Day of Atonement, which is accompanied by fasting and confession of sins. Sukkot, the Jewish harvest festival, follows. At the end of Sukkot there is Simchat Torah, the rejoicing of the Law, when the yearly cycle of the reading of the Law is completed and started again. Simchat Torah is further marked by the ceremonial carrying the scrolls of the Law seven times around the synagogue.

During October, the harvest festivals that began in the previous month may continue. One notable harvest festival that takes place regularly in October is the Oktoberfest in Munich to celebrate the completion of the hop harvest.

In China there is the Chong Yang festival, on the ninth day of the ninth moon, when it is traditional for Chinese people to climb pagodas or hills. This is done in commemoration of a family who were told they would avoid disaster on this day if they took refuge up in the hills.

The Hindu festival of Dusshera, or Durga-puja, is celebrated at this time, during a period known as Navaratri (Nine Nights). This is a ten-day celebration in honour of the goddess Durga. Huge figures of demons, filled with explosives and fireworks, are set alight.

In the Christian West, October ends with All Souls' Day and the traditions of Hallowe'en. All Souls' Day is the time at which Christians traditionally pray for the souls of the dead. Hallowe'en may have its origins in the ancient Celtic New Year festival of Samhain, with which it coincides. Now, especially in North America and increasingly in western Europe, children dress up as witches or ghosts, and play 'trick or treat'.

For Americans, November is the time of Thanksgiving, celebrated with a traditional meal of turkey, cranberry jelly and pumpkin pie. This is also the time of the Christian All Saints' Day and the Mexican Day of the Dead. On Armistice Day many countries honour those who have lost their lives in war. Finally, November is the time of Diwali, the spectacular Hindu festival of lights.

November

The Christian celebration of All Souls' Day is a prelude to All Saints' Day (1 November), celebrating all the Christian saints. This is a day on which saints who do not have a specific day for their commemoration are remembered. In some countries, All Souls' Day is celebrated on 2 November. This is the Mexican Day of the Dead, a time of all-night vigils at gravesides, of cakes and sweets made in the shape of skulls, of the lighting of candles in memory of the dead. The following day there is a feast.

The lighting of lamps is also something that characterizes Diwali, the Hindu festival of lights. The festival is held to honour Lakshmi, the goddess of wealth. Patterns of rice flour are made on doorsteps and homes are decorated with many little clay oil lamps called *divas*, which are also lit in the temples and out in the streets. Every Hindu household celebrates Diwali, and India is ablaze with flickering lights for two days.

For the Sikhs, November is the time to celebrate the birthday of Guru Nanak, the founder of their religion. The Sikhs also celebrate Diwali, in honour of their Guru Hargobind. The Golden Temple is brilliantly illuminated at night.

Lights of a different kind burn in England, where 5 November is Guy Fawkes' Night. This commemorates the unsuccessful attempt in 1605 by Guy Fawkes and a group of conspirators to blow up the Houses of Parliament. Effigies of 'the Guy' are burnt on bonfires, and fireworks light up the sky in a possible extension of the tradition of lighting of Hallowe'en or Samhain fires.

In America, the end of November is enlivened by Thanksgiving, which began as an August harvest festival and was moved to November in 1863. Now it is held as a way of thanking God for all his blessings.

CANDLES FOR CHRISTMAS AND WINTER
Christmas is a rich amalgam of pagan and Christian festivities. The lighting of candles, decorating of evergreen trees, and the carrying of wreaths recall an ancient pagan past. Customs, such as the singing of carols, bring the Christian religion to the forefront of the celebrations. And other traditions like that of present-giving, while relating to Christian ideas, have taken on a secular life of their own.

December

For thousands of years people in the northern hemisphere have been celebrating the winter solstice and warming themselves to face the rain, wind and snow of December. The winter solstice was celebrated in the old Roman feast of Saturnalia, a period of licence and merrymaking. The Germanic peoples celebrated 'Yule', the feast of the god Jolnir (or Thor), when the Yule log was burned. Although there was no reason to suppose that Christ was actually born at the winter solstice, the old pagan celebrations were taken over by the Christians in the 4th century.

Nowadays this is a time of celebration all over the Christian world, with present-giving, the eating of special celebratory foods, the decoration of homes with paper streamers and Christmas trees, and the singing of carols.

In the month when candles are alight in Christian homes, Jews light candles for Chanukah, the festival that commemorates Jewish victories over the invading Syrians. The celebrations last for eight days, because when the temple was retaken, it was said that a lamp inside burned for eight days, even though it contained only a single day's supply of oil. Like Christmas, Chanukah is also a time of present-giving.

The Swedish celebrate St Lucia's day on 13 December, which is said to be the longest, darkest night in Sweden. Young girls with crowns of candles lead the celebrations, and candle-lit feasts are traditionally held at dawn.

The Chinese winter solstice festival is Dong Zhi. Memories of the dead are conjured up at the time of the dying year, and places are left for the spirits of ancestors at Dong Zhi feasts.

In Japan, light of a more symbolic kind, is evoked in the Zen festival of the enlightenment of the Buddha. It is a period of concentrated meditation, in which it is hoped to imitate Buddha's search for enlightenment.

DEVELOPING

FROM CRADLE TO GRAVE: RITES OF PASSAGE

Birth, coming of age, marriage, death. Whoever we are and wherever we live, we cannot avoid these great climaxes and crises of life. People need to ease these changes in a number of ways. And a change in status needs to be made known to the community. Rituals to signal and mark these key life changes – rites of passage, as they are called – occur in all human societies and they seem to fulfil a basic human need.

Common elements

Rites of passage from all over the world have many common elements. To take examples from birth ceremonies: in both Muslim and Sikh rituals sweet food is placed on the mouth of the baby; both Chinese and Hindu births are traditionally greeted with the casting of a horoscope. Marriages, from China to the Muslim countries, are the occasion of exchange of gifts between the two famiIes; both Hindu and Sikh weddings involve physically tying the couple together. And similarities continue in the final rituals of death: most funerals involve washing the body and covering it in special clothing.
There is also a common structure that can be seen in many rites of passage. The early 20th-century Belgian anthropologist and folklorist Arnold van Gennep divided the rites into three phases: separation, transition and reincorporation. First, the person is cut off from his or her old role. Next there is a period of adjustment and transition from one status to the next; this often involves some sort of physical transformation. Finally the person rejoins society with a new social status.

The continuing need

Historically, these ceremonies have often been religious rites. They have been, and often still are, presided over by a priest or priestess, and they may take place on sacred ground. The sanction and authority of religion has traditionally given a special power to rites of passage. Nowadays, with society in large parts of the globe becoming more secular, this sanction is diminishing. But even in secular societies, individuals still need to mark these key points in their lives. This need is also seen in the wider social effects of the rituals. By relieving the stress within a community that can surround change, they help to prevent social disruption. By bringing people together, they foster co-operation. By providing clear instructions to individuals, they help people to live up to society's expectations. Rites of passage remain one of the most basic and most fascinating expressions of human culture.

Childbirth

For many parents, the birth of a child is the most important event of their lives. It is also a time of physical challenge for the mother and emotional challenge for both parents. It is an event that holds great mystery and yet is entirely natural and essential to secure our survival as a species.

The delights and challenges of childbirth are such that it is only to be expected that this momentous event should be accompanied with some of the most elaborate rites of passage. The birth itself may be a very private affair, in many societies the preserve of the women alone. But many different people are often involved, directly or indirectly, in the rituals surrounding it.

As with other rituals and customs that take place at the turning points of our lives, what happens is as important for society as a whole as for the individual at the centre of the ceremony. In this case the newborn baby, unaware of such events, will only later appreciate the significance of the formal marking of his or her arrival.

PREPARATION

For the mother, adjustment has to begin well before the birth itself. Carrying a child is in itself hard work, particularly in the later stages of pregnancy. In many societies this is recognized: a preganant woman is encouraged to reduce her normal activities and to take more rest. But this is by no means universal. Among the !Kung of the Kalahari Desert in southern Africa, the women are the main food providers and a pregnant !Kung woman will often carry on the job of food gathering, coming home with as large a load as her sisters.

Indeed food is important during pregnancy – it is not only the modern western nutritionist who knows this. Many societies recognize that the mother should pay particular attention to maintaining a balanced diet. Different cultures express this in different ways: a Chinese doctor will talk of a balance between *yin* and *yang* foods; a midwife from northern India, following the

WELCOME!
In many societies the new baby is lifted up for all to see as a ritual of acceptance.

tenets of Ayurvedic medicine, might recommend 'hot' and 'cold' foods in equal proportions. A midwife in northern India may advise the woman against eating gifts of rich sweetmeats from her family – on the basis that her weakened constitution might not be able to cope with such foods. The western physician will almost certainly recommend a ban on smoking and drinking alcohol, which could harm the baby.

In Central America dietary recommendations are also sometimes couched in terms of hot and cold. A pregnant woman in Guatemala is said to be in a very 'hot' state and so should avoid foods that are considered to be too hot (oregano, honey and certain green vegetables, for example). On the other hand, she is also told to avoid very 'cold' foods (such as beans, pork and fizzy drinks), since her very heat puts her at risk from attacks of cold.

In addition, the Guatemalan woman is told to respect her dietary cravings. These are seen as representing the wishes of the baby and denying them can lead to a miscarriage.

Finally, there is advice on particular foods to avoid. Rabbit meat (linked with multiple births) and twinned fruit, like the chayote, (associated with twins) are two examples. The belief that the outward shape or characteristics of a food are thought to relate to their effects on the eater, is a common concept in many cultures. Pregnant Inuit women are told not to chew spruce gum or chewing gum, which may make the placenta stick to the mother's womb.

In many societies, pregnant women undergo another type of preparation, learning as much as they can about the process of childbirth itself and about how to bring up a young baby. In the West, many women attend ante-natal classes, where they learn about the process of birth and the basics of caring for a newborn baby. In traditional societies, the task of preparing the mother for the birth is usually taken on by the older women of the family or village. Alternatively, there may be a local

ANTICIPATING THE BIRTH
Mothers all over the world view the imminent arrival of a new baby with a mixture of excitement and trepidation.

midwife, versed in traditional and sometimes modern medical skills, who can instruct and advise new mothers.

CONFINEMENT AND BIRTH

All over the world – from the Navaho of North America to adherants of the Shinto religion in Japan – birth has traditionally taken place in relative seclusion, usually in the presence only of women. This has many advantages: it removes the woman from her everyday roles and gives her the time and space to concentrate on the birth. In many societies it is felt that it is wrong for men to know too much about the process of childbirth, and that if they do, the 'magic' and 'mystery' of the event could be put in jeopardy.

Often there may also be a long period of confinement after the birth has taken place. Such a period not only enables the mother to

REMOVING INAUSPICIOUSNESS

Sometimes the problems of pregnancy and childbirth are countered by carrying out a spiritual ritual. In northern India the complex sequence of rituals described here is regularly performed to ensure the good fortune of mother and child and to protect them from the influence of malign ancestor gods. Each ritual involves transferring the ill omen from one person to another, away from the confinement room, so that the new arrival may start life in the most favourable way possible.

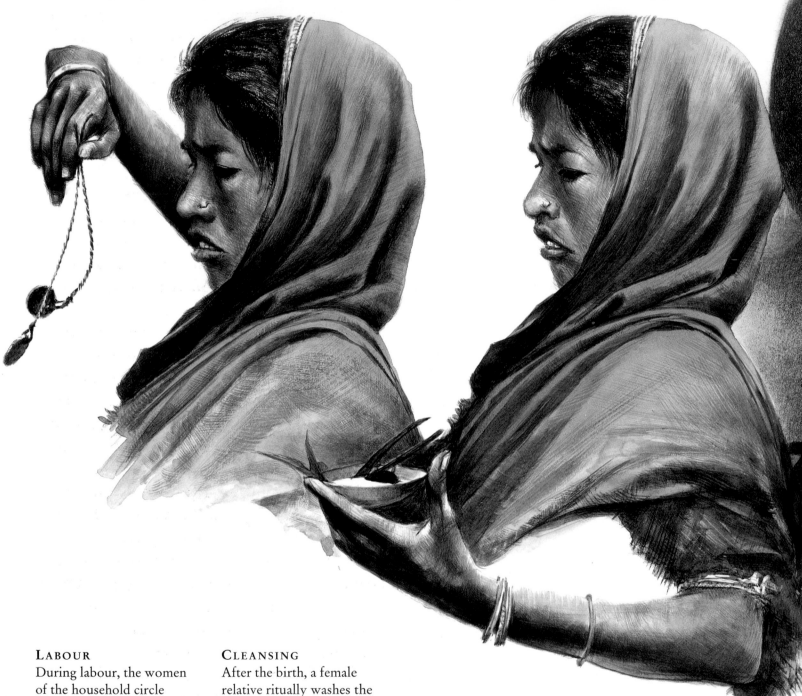

LABOUR

During labour, the women of the household circle coins (one rupee and one-and-a quarter rupee pieces) over the mother. This procedure is believed to speed up the delivery and to take away any danger from malign spirits. The coins are removed to a safe place and later given to the wife of the Brahman (priest).

CLEANSING

After the birth, a female relative ritually washes the mother's breasts to purify them. She then brings a small saucer of milk and blades of grass in which she places a coin. She sprinkles the milk on the mother's breasts, using the blades of grass. When she has finished, she takes the coin away with her, again to remove the influence of dangerous ancestor-gods.

OFFERINGS

Another important ritual occurs on the sixth day after the birth. The midwife returns to the confinement room and performs a ceremony to the goddess Bemata, who is believed to have placed the baby in the mother's womb. Grain is placed on a tray and covered with a cloth. Sugar and flour are set on another tray. A lamp filled with mustard oil is placed at the head end of the cot and five

recover from the physical ordeal of childbirth before resuming normal life, but also allows bonding between mother and child to take place unhindered by normal day-to-day responsibilities. Sometimes this is achieved by setting aside a special building for the birth, sometimes by the mother disappearing into the countryside, sometimes by sending the men away during the period leading up to the birth.

In some parts of West Africa, the mother traditionally enjoyed complete seclusion. The anthropologist Northcote Thomas, writing at the beginning of this century, noted that in some tribes the woman disappeared off into the bush to give birth, often unattended.

Nevertheless, it is more common for birth to take place in the company of other women. Among the Tukano Indians of the Amazon, for example, birth takes place in the field, in the presence of the father's mother and sometimes a blood relative of the mother. In Borneo traditionally birth takes place in seclusion, with the woman hidden from her husband by a screen of mats; the arrival of the baby was announced by the beating of a drum.

In Madagascar it is also traditional for the birth to take place in a room partitioned off from the main house. The mother is attended by older women who act as midwives. But the confinement is not completely private. Friends and relatives who have been told of the birth arrive to visit the mother and bring gifts. Often they bring money, which was traditionally intended to buy firewood, for Malagasy women believe heat to be advantageous during labour. Traditionally a fire is lit in the delivery room even at the warmest times of the year.

In the Punjab the mother is usually attended by the village midwife, her mother or mother-in-law and perhaps her father's sister-in-law. Nowadays, the midwife's traditional skills are often supplemented by training in modern midwifery.

While in the vast majority of traditional societies men are excluded from childbirth, in

heaps of fried bread are laid out, one for each leg of the cot, one for the goddess. A rough image of Bemata is made of cow dung and wrapped in cloth. Some of the grain is handed to the mother as she squats down by the cot with the child in her arms. Then she makes an offering to the goddess. The items used in the ritual are later taken away by the midwife, thereby removing any remaining ill fortune.

some places it is thought acceptable, or even advantageous, for the father to be present. Among the Kalmyk Mongols, for example, the father and other males attend the labour up until the moment of birth. In many western societies, women gave birth apart from their husbands until comparatively recently. But it is now accepted that a male partner has a role in helping the western mother during labour.

The Dangers of Childbirth

The accounts of early anthropologists are often enviously full of accounts of easy birth among people living in traditional societies. Later researchers, however, have observed that this view may be misleading. In Australia, where early accounts suggested that birth was nearly always easy and straightforward, with no

Pollution and childbirth in New Guinea

The Hua people of the highlands of New Guinea hold strongly to the concept of female impurity or pollution. Hua men are particularly anxious about the effects of pollution from menstrual blood and the fluids associated with childbirth. When these are expelled from the female body, the woman is considered to lose some of her pollution, but the danger is that this can be transferred to someone else. A newly married woman is considered highly polluted, and no male or postmenopausal woman of her husband's community is allowed to eat any food that she has made or served. But she becomes less polluted with the birth of each child and by old age may have got rid of all of her pollution.

Diet
Specific foods are recommended either to be eaten or avoided by Hua women who are pregnant. These dietary rules are intended to counter pollution and to ensure a straightforward labour. Greasy or slippery foods – for example, pig fat, frogs, a particularly juicy species of the vegetable *Amaranthus*, and various types of mushrooms – are supposed to speed up delivery and help the child slip out of the womb easily. By contrast, foods that might make the womb dry out (types of yam and banana) are to be avoided. So are burned tubers, which might make the baby stick in the womb, just as the food sticks to the cooking pot.

Easing the birth
Other measures to encourage 'slipperiness' are taken during labour to speed up the birth. The woman sits in water, which is supposed to go up into the womb, making the baby wet and slippery. To help matters further, a spell is recited over the mother.

The nursing mother
There are other dietary recommendations for nursing mothers. Particular foods, such as pig fat, water, sugarcane, cucumber, are prescribed to encourage the flow of milk. Observing these recommendations is not so important, however, if the mother's milk is flowing well.

confinement period, they have shown that there is in fact often a period of confinement, during which men and unmarried girls are excluded from the presence of the mother. The Aborigines themselves stress that birth is not always easy, and they use special songs to help the process along. Such accounts remind us that in traditional societies there is just as much likelihood of pain and complications as in our own – although women in such cultures often bear these problems with little complaint.

In some cultures the dangers of birth are emphasized much more strongly. The African Lele people, for example, look upon childbirth with great anxiety. Both mother and unborn child are held to be in danger and are considered to be under the influence of forest spirits who hold sway over both childbirth and hunting. Societies that believe in female 'pollution' (see Re-entering society, page 52) also emphasize the dangers of childbirth. It may even be the unborn child who is believed to pose a danger to others. A pregnant Lele woman, for example, will avoid approaching a sick person, lest their illness be made worse by the unborn child.

Similarly, many South American peoples, such as the Makuna of the northwestern Amazon, take special precautions against dangerous spirits, who are believed to threaten the birth. Before the birth, the father asks the local shaman (priest or medicine man) to perform birth magic. This helps to shield the parents and newborn baby from the influence of evil spririts and thereby ensures that the baby will be healthy.

Couvade

In some cultures there is the custom of couvade. This has been recorded in various places, from Guyana to Melanesia, and to southern India. The idea is that the father undergoes a confinement similar to that of the mother. So strong was the tradition of couvade

CLOSE CONTACT
The bond between mother and child, reinforced by close physical contact, is common to all peoples from the African !Kung, who carry even quite large children when out gathering food, to the western 'nuclear' family.

RITUAL BLESSING
Babies everywhere are brought to spiritual leaders
to be blessed or named. Here a southern African
shaman (witch doctor) performs the ritual.

in some places that it even replaced the confinement of the mother. In Guyana, for example, the mother would work hard until labour was imminent, give birth, and then be back at her normal everyday work very soon afterwards. The father, on the other hand, would be confined to bed. In these societies, fathers who practise couvade are seen as taking as vital a part in the birth as western men who nowadays stay with their partners to offer support during labour.

During the couvade the father may be given a restricted diet (an extract of manioc meal was traditional in Guyana), and forbidden to smoke, wash or touch tools or weapons; he may even be nursed by the women of the village. The father must adhere strictly to these rules to ensure the baby's health.

RE-ENTERING SOCIETY

In many societies, after the relative isolation of the birth, the mother undergoes a form of reintroduction into the community. In England the religious ceremony known as the 'churching of women' fulfilled this function. In this ritual, the woman gave thanks to God for

delivering her from, in the words of the Anglican *Book of Common Prayer*, 'the pain and peril of childbirth'. Although this ceremony is less common now, some mothers who are in hospital on a Sunday after giving birth will still be asked if they would like to visit the hospital chapel to give thanks to God.

Elsewhere, rituals marking a woman's reintegration into society are linked to the concept of impurity or pollution: a woman is held to be in some way impure during the period immediately before and after birth. This belief is particularly strong among some New Guinea peoples – the Hua, for example (see page 48). This set of beliefs also has implications for the children. The babies – who are the means by which the mother is purified – are themselves considered to be polluted and are seen to pose a threat to those who come into contact with them. The firstborn child is considered the most polluted of all. It is said that a Hua father would never touch his firstborn child, but would poke it playfully with a stick.

In many cultures the new mother undergoes a ritual cleansing before coming out of confinement and returning to normal

CHILDBIRTH AMONG THE MAASAI

At the beginning of the pregnancy, a Maasai woman eats a normal diet, although she responds to any cravings. As the pregnancy advances, she may change her diet – for example, she may avoid milk, which may make the baby too fat, resulting in a difficult delivery. She also avoids the meat of any diseased animal. In addition, she will eat only well-cooked meat, thus reducing the risk of infection by parasites – a precaution that meets with the approval of both traditional and scientific medicine.

THE BIRTH

The baby is born at home. The midwife is usually an older woman from the mother's own family. When the baby has been delivered, the midwife cuts the cord, saying 'You are now responsible for your life, as I am responsible for mine'. The mother and child are washed with a mixture of water and milk.

BOY OR GIRL?

The father is not allowed near while the mother is giving birth. Afterwards, the midwife calls to him and, if the child is a girl, tells him to draw blood from the jugular vein of a heifer and to make a half-hearted or mock attempt to do the same from a bullock. The instructions are reversed for a boy.

FEASTS AND BLESSINGS

The blood that the father brings is mixed with milk to make a drink for the mother. Then a ram is slaughtered inside the mother's house and eaten by the assembled women. After the feast, the women sing prayers blessing the child, the mother, the house, and the whole family. On the next day, a sheep is slaughtered. The midwife is given the best cuts of meat, and the fat is melted down to make a drink for the mother.

NAMING

In some Maasai communities the child's naming ceremony follows soon after. The mother dresses in her best skirt of lambskin decorated with beads, together with bead earrings and necklaces. The elders and women decide on a name for the child and bless the baby with the words 'May that name dwell in you.'

society. In Palau, Micronesia, there is a short but intense period of isolation for the mother after she has given birth. She lives apart for four days, and on each day the midwife ritually bathes her eight times. On each occasion she is annointed with coconut oil mixed with turmeric and rubbed with rebotel leaves. Only after this process is completed is she deemed ready to return to society.

Among Hindus in India, the duration of a woman's impurity depends on her caste: from 10 days, for members of the priestly Brahman caste, to up to 40 days for the lower castes. However, for all women, regardless of caste, the total time of the confinement is normally 40 days. This means that a Brahman woman is therby confined for a period far longer than that of her impurity. After this confinement, the mother and baby visit the temple, where both are blessed and the baby's name is chosen.

Some anthropologists have seen the idea of pollution mirrored in modern western attitudes to birth. Here, the mother is often seen by the medical establishment as someone who is 'ill' and 'in need of treatment'. This attitude seems to be confirmed by the emphasis on the dangers of childbirth and the way in which the mother is surrounded with monitoring equipment in the delivery room.

A move away from the association of pregnancy with illness is shown by the natural childbirth movement in the West, which stresses the positive aspects of birth. Indeed, many traditional attitudes to childbirth in the West emphasize these positive attitudes, even seeing a woman's true entry into adult society as dating from her first confinement. Amish women (those belonging to a German-speaking Mennonite sect in the United States), for example, see birth as an experience that confirms their role in society, and there is no question of any associated pollution.

In societies that practise couvade, both parents need to rejoin normal society. Among the Buka people of the Solomon Islands, on the fourth day after the birth the father goes to see his wife and baby and is then allowed to wander around the village, but not to work, hunt or fish. For some time after the birth, neither parent is allowed to eat meat or fish. One reason given for this is that eating these foods would harm the child. But the prohibition also compensates for the fact that the father is still not allowed to hunt, and so the meat and fish supply in the village may be reduced. Eventually, the parents are allowed to resume their normal diet and the father may hunt once more.

NAMING

The newborn baby is not instantly and automatically a member of society. His or her entry into society is usually marked by some special ceremony. In some cases this might be little more than a formal announcement that the birth has taken place. Thus the Herero people of southern Africa announced the arrival of a boy with a cry of 'Okauta' ('a little bow'); the arrival of a girl was greeted with 'Okazeu' (the name of one of the bulbs which the women gather for food). Often the birth of a baby is marked by a more elaborate ritual. In Japan, the new baby was ceremonially taken to visit the temple, given presents including a protective toy dog, and fed a ritual 'first meal'. The formal acceptance of the new infant as a

ENTERING SOCIETY
Naming rituals allow a baby formally to take his or her place in society.

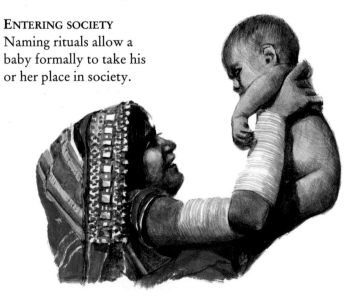

BIRTH CUSTOMS OF THE NAVAHO

For Navaho women traditional birth took place in the hogan (earth-covered wooden cabin). Before birth, there were important customs to follow and prohibitions to observe. The mother must not tie knots or the baby will get tangled up with the umbilical cord. She must not turn work on her loom upside-down or a breech birth would occur.

THE START OF LABOUR

At the beginning of labour the mother drank a herbal tea. The husband sprinkled sand on the floor and old cloths or a sheep skin were laid on the sand. The woman knelt down on this covering, let her hair down, and removed her jewellery. A red sash sprinkled with pollen was hung from the roof over her head for her to hold during labour.

HASTENING THE BIRTH

If the labour was long, the other women would let down their hair. In addition, the midwife would knead the mother's abdomen and rub her with pollen or even hold her upside down. A singer might perform a song and beckon the baby out with an eagle-feather brush.

THE ARRIVAL OF THE BABY

For the birth, one woman knelt in front to hold the baby, while another held the mother from behind. The father might press the mother's abdomen, to push the baby out.

FIRST BATH

After the placenta was expelled and the cord cut, the woman who received the baby gave it its first bath. Then the child was wrapped up in sheepskin or cloth and placed next to its mother, with its head towards the fire. The baby's head was anointed with pollen.

SHAPING THE BABY

The woman who bathed the baby then 'moulded' the nose, head and limbs of the baby. This ritual ensured healthy growth and that the child would have a straight nose, long limbs, and so on.

member of society frequently involves a ritual in which the child is given a name. The ceremony can identify the child and make public his or her parentage. It may also signal the child's entry into the local religion, and magic may be performed to protect the child from evil spirits. The ritual may lay down the responsibilities of the parents and others in looking after the child. In some cases, the naming ceremony also serves to mark the return of the mother to normal society after her confinement.

Often the naming ritual re-enacts the birth in some way – the child is reborn into society. This is the case in religions such as Christianity, where water is a vital part of the process. In some churches, the infant is immersed in water before being held up for the congregation to see. This has reminded some writers of a symbolic death by drowning followed by a rebirth. For others it is a recreation of the actual birth. There is also a more literal reminder of Christ's own baptism in the River Jordan. In many churches total immersion has been abandoned in favour of splashing water on the infant's head.

The elemental aspect of the Christian use of water in this way, is also seen in other cultures that use other basic elements to welcome their newborn into the community. Among the

CIRCUMCISION

Boys and young men are circumcised in many different cultures. Jewish boys are circumcised very early - traditionally on the eighth day of the baby's life. Among Jews, circumcision is a response to the text of Genesis 17:10: 'every man child among you shall be circumcised'. Circumcision thus confirms the obligation to live according to the law of God.

THE CEREMONY

In Europe and the United States, the ceremony usually takes place in the home, or in hospital. Some Jews carry out circumcision in the synagogue. The boy is given to his godfather who recites with the assembled men a greeting in Hebrew: 'Blessed be he that cometh'. The godfather then sits down with the child on his knees and the company prays as the circumcision takes place. The operation is traditionally performed by an official called a *mohel*, though nowadays it is more likely to be carried out by a doctor. After the circumcision the child receives his name.

Blood Indians of North America, for example, earth and sun are key elements in the ritual. The elder uses red ochre to to mark the palm of his hand and to paint the sign of the tribe on the baby's face. He then holds the baby high in his arms, showing the child to the sun, in the hope that its light will always follow the child as it grows up.

For other cultures, fire is the important purifying and protective element. Some Australian Aborigines practise 'baby smoking'. A fire of konkerberry leaves and twigs is lit and dampened bark and green leaves are thrown onto the fire to make smoke. Then the child's mother squeezes milk onto the fire and the grandmother passes the baby through the smoke. The participation of the mother and grandmother gives the child the protection of its relatives; the use of the konkerberry leaves provides protection from the land itself.

Other types of ceremony can mark the baby's welcome into the community. In the Jewish faith, for example, circumcision is performed on the eighth day of a boy's life, at which time he also receives his name. The operation is intended to signal the Jew's obligation to live a virtuous life and to observe and teach God's law.

The role of the father and the male relatives is often important in naming and similar ceremonies, providing the opportunity to assert and confirm the child's paternity.

The choice of name can also carry great significance. Names are powerful symbols, and draw a special sort of attention to their bearers. In Borneo it was the tradition not to name a child for the first few years of its life. It was feared that to give it a name would draw the attention of evil spirits to the newborn. If a child suffered ill health or bad luck after being named, it was not uncommon for the name to be changed to divert the malign spirits.

Most peoples have conventions that influence how the name is chosen. These vary widely. There is a tradition in Burma that

ADOPTION IN CHINA
Among the rich families of traditional Chinese society, it is thought almost essential for a man to produce a son to carry on the male line and worship the spirits of his ancestors. In the absence of a natural son, therefore, it is not uncommon for Chinese people to adopt a boy from another family.

CHOOSING AN HEIR
There are specific (mainly unwritten) rules governing the choice of an adoptive son. The man is expected to select from kin on his father's side of the family. If there are no available heirs among his brothers or their sons, he should look next among the descendants of his grandfather, and so on. Providing the man is able to offer his heir a secure future, the boy's family is likely to consent. Adoption beyond the level of brothers has to be accompanied by a lavish banquet, during which all the elders place their signatures on a banner of red cloth, to indicate that the adoption is legitimate.

RITUAL INSULTS
If a man is forced to adopt from outside his own family by buying an heir, an even larger banquet is held. During this, the guests humiliate the father by hurling insults at him, mentioning his inability to provide an heir of his own.

infants are named according to astrological principles, with names beginning with particular letters allotted to specific days of the week. Names used to be chosen after the consultation of a horoscope in Thailand. In some cultures it is customary to name a child after a living relative, in others this is taboo.

In Bali the personal names of the majority of the population are nonsense-syllables that bear no relation to any other names. Within each settlement all the personal names are different, they indicate no family connections, and are not nicknames. In other words, each person's name is unique to that individual and

is a very personal piece of property – so much so, indeed, that these names are rarely used out loud, and it is not unknown for an elderly Balinese person to be the only one who knows his name. Young people are more likely to be known by another name, which they are given at the moment of birth and which indicates whether they are first, second, third, and so on, in the family. Adults are known by a public or status-group title.

Among the Navaho people of North America, the name is a gift that can be bestowed on the child by a relative. Sometimes the mother names the daughters, the father the

THE CHILD AND THE SPIRIT WORLD – RITUALS FOR PROTECTION

In many cultures there are special customs and ceremonies to protect the child in its vulnerable early days. Many of these are designed to ward off the actions of evil spirits – and to allay parental anxieties about the health and good fortune of the new baby.

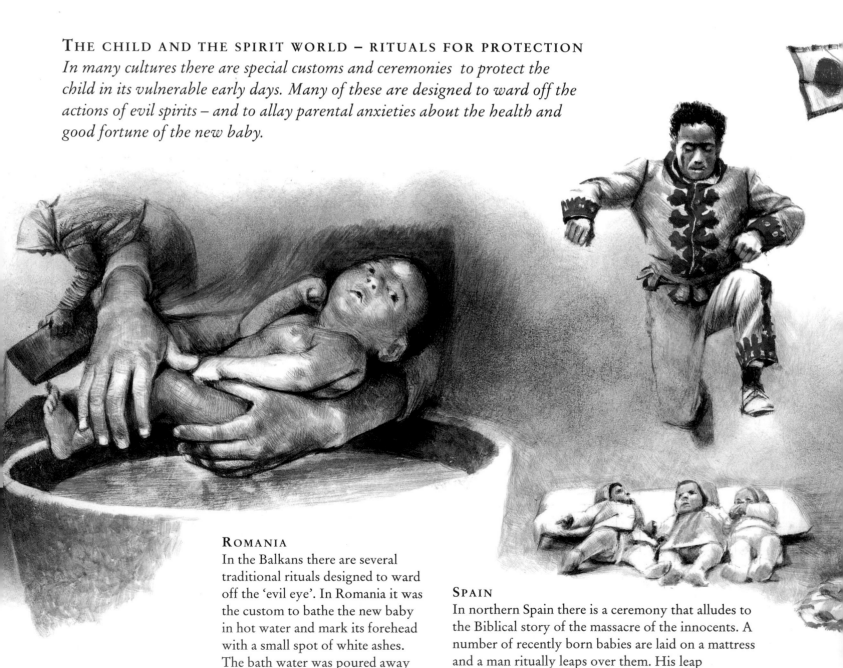

ROMANIA
In the Balkans there are several traditional rituals designed to ward off the 'evil eye'. In Romania it was the custom to bathe the new baby in hot water and mark its forehead with a small spot of white ashes. The bath water was poured away carefully in some clean place, to avoid spilling it on the fates.

SPAIN
In northern Spain there is a ceremony that alludes to the Biblical story of the massacre of the innocents. A number of recently born babies are laid on a mattress and a man ritually leaps over them. His leap symbolizes the danger the children face, his successful landing on the ground, their escape from that danger.

sons. Or the mother can give the right of naming to a sister to whom she is particularly close, and that sister can give her name to the child. But the namer does not have to give his or her own name to the child; it can be the name of a deceased relative. It is considered particularly auspicious to give a child the name of someone who lived to an old age.

In many places the celebration and naming of the child is quite a small ceremony, attended only by close relatives. But this is by no means always the case. In Uganda, for example, the tradition was for the whole village to celebrate with singing and dancing. The father would walk round the groups of villagers and receive congratulations. The mother and child would stay at the entrance to their house, and people would come up one by one to congratulate her. Eventually people would gather around the mother and child and the eldest grandfather would lift the child up and speak its name. In all societies the customs and rituals surrounding childbirth help those involved with the birth to take on board its significance, overcome its perils and take pleasure in its joys. They help parents to cope with the new arrival and ease these individuals back into society after the birth.

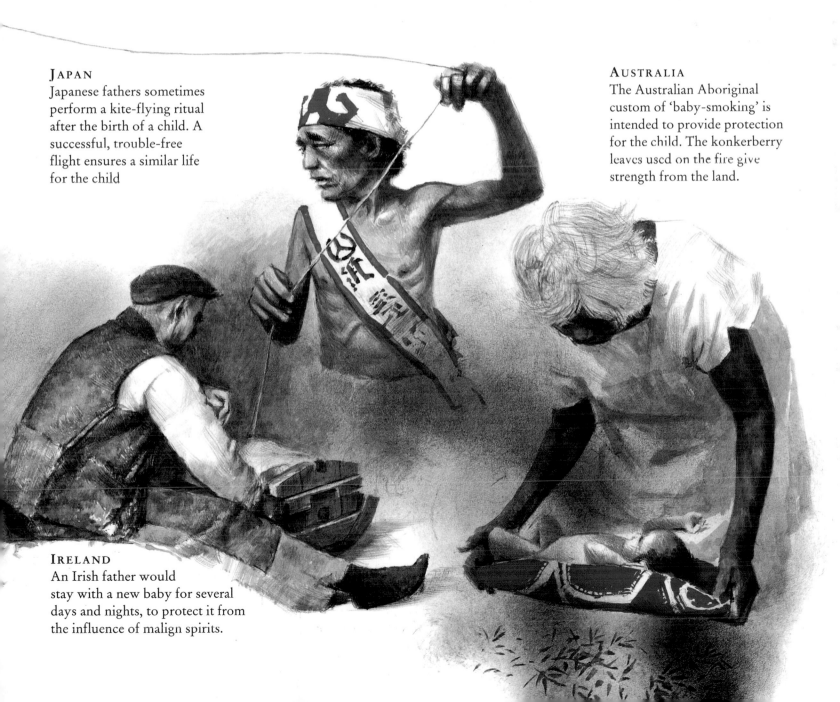

JAPAN
Japanese fathers sometimes perform a kite-flying ritual after the birth of a child. A successful, trouble-free flight ensures a similar life for the child

AUSTRALIA
The Australian Aboriginal custom of 'baby-smoking' is intended to provide protection for the child. The konkerberry leaves used on the fire give strength from the land.

IRELAND
An Irish father would stay with a new baby for several days and nights, to protect it from the influence of malign spirits.

Coming of age

In nearly every society there is some ritual to mark the individual's passage from childhood to adulthood. Such ceremonies can take many forms. In many traditional societies the young person undergoes some form of bodily ordeal (often involving mutilation or marking of the body). In addition, the ritual may have some educational content to prepare the individual for adult life.

It is sometimes said that coming-of-age ceremonies are uncommon in Western industrialized societies, particularly as religious rituals like Protestant confirmation are less frequently observed than in the past. But there are other rituals, albeit simple ones, that mark this rite of passage in the West.

In England, for example, when a young person reached the age of 21, there was a ritual of handing over the key of the door to signify that he or she had been given the right to come and go as he or she pleased.

In North America, where people define their adult freedom partly in terms of the ownership and use of a car, The transition from childhood to adulthood is likely to be symbolized by the acquisition of a driver's licence or the handing over of a set of car keys.

In traditional societies, survival depends on a person's ability to obtain food. So among the !Kung hunter-gatherers of the Kalahari desert a young man's entry into the adult world coincides with his first kill on the hunt. While with the Yupik of Alaska, the same importance is attached to a boy's killing his first seal. Other traditional societies, like the Dani of Indonesia, incorporated mock battles into their coming-of-age rituals.

Many societies include instruction in the female role for their adolescent girls. Young women of the Mendi people of Sierra Leone,

for example, spend time in the bush being inducted into the Bundu society, to which traditionally most women belong. The ceremony takes place in seclusion in the bush, and involves the learning of special dances, as well as preparation for married life.

Many of the young women are already betrothed, but will be considered fit for marriage only when they have joined the Bundu and been given the basic women's education that this provides.

Another example of this educational aspect of coming-of-age ceremonies is the introduction to basic agricultural techniques thatoften takes place in southern India. Here, the young person will be shown how to milk their first buffalo on an auspicious day or on New Year's Day.

THE IDEA OF INITIATION

The rituals that mark coming of age are often referred to as initiation ceremonies – they admit the candidate into a new social sphere from which he or she was previously excluded. But such ceremonies of initiation occur at a very wide range of different ages. It is well known, for example, that the Jews and many Muslims circumcise male babies when they are a few days old (see page 56), while for many other peoples, circumcision is a signal of entry into adulthood and is performed during adolescence. There can be wide variations of timing even within a single race or narrow geographical area. Anthropologists studying Morocco at the end of the last century, for example, found the ritual of circumcision performed at the ages of seven days to 13 years in Dukalla, between two and ten years at Fez, at eight years at Tangiers, from two to four years around Mogador, and at other times in other locations.

Clearly not all of these differently timed cimcumcision rituals can be rites of entry into adulthood. Just as circumcision for the Jews is a sign both of the collective covenant with their God and that the individual child belongs this religious group, so the ritual creates a similar sign of belonging in many other cultures. It is thus similar to other childhood ceremonies such as naming ceremonies, ritual first haircuts, and ceremonies carried out when a child is teething, that mark out the young person as part of a particular social set.

TIMING

The precise time in the individual's life at which rituals of coming of age are performed varies greatly from place to place. It is clear is that coming of age in a social sense does necessarily not take place at the onset of physical puberty. This would be difficult in many societies in which the rituals are

GRADUATION CEREMONIES
Nowadays the path to adulthood is often measured by milestones in a person's education. High-school leaving rituals and college graduation ceremonies therefore take on a particular significance.

LEAVING SCHOOL
Hungarian secondary school leavers embark on their adult lives. The dark-suited youths carry bunches of flowers – good luck presents from their parents, relatives and friends.

UNIVERSITY GRADUATION
Students at an English university wear black gowns with hoods decorated in different colours or fabrics to indicate the degree they have been awarded. Some of these ceremonies include processions and Latin orations.

DRESSING FOR ADULTHOOD
Rituals of coming of age usually involve special costumes. A white confirmation veil or novice monk's habit indicates purity; a painted face can represent adult power or a symbolic 'death' before rebirth into adulthood. The young Buddhist's saffron robes show that he is learning to observe the disciplines of his religion.

collective, because the outward signs of puberty appear at different dates for different individuals. In addition, coming-of-age ceremonies often have several stages extending over a long period of time. This would again make it impossible to link the ceremony to a precise point of physiological development.

True, there is often an individual ceremony performed for women at their first menses. But this can have more to do with notions of impurity than with coming of age, and there may well be a separate coming-of-age ceremony performed at some other time.

Choice of time, then, may be related to the young person's age or to some other pointer. For example, among some native North American peoples a young man's coming-of-age ceremony can take place after his first dream of an arrow, or a canoe, or a woman. For the !Kung, the rules are different for the two sexes. A woman is often married by the time she is 16 or 17 years old, the average time of first menses among this people. Even so, the onset of menstruation does not indicate that a !Kung girl will start to assume an adult role. The older women of her family (her mother

and in-laws) may well still help her in her day-to-day duties in the household and she may continue to play with her friends for much of the day. It is not until she has her first child that the young woman is considered truly an adult !Kung men often have to wait until they are between 20 or 30 to get married and, their initiation into manhood is triggered by their first hunting kill, which can be expected to occur at a time when they have achieved a certain level of experience and skill in the hunt.

The cost of the ceremony may also affect the timing. Among the Maasai people of East Africa boys, usually come of age between the ages of 12 and 16. But if the parents cannot afford the ceremony, it may be put off until they can; a child whose family is rich might be initiated at an earlier age. In addition, a Maasai child has to wait until a collective ceremony takes place – they normally only occur every four or five years. Finally, the father of a candidate for initiation will himself have had to have been through certain rituals before his child can come of age. From this example, we can clearly see the distinction between physical puberty and social coming of age.

THE GENERAL PATTERN

As with other rites of passage, coming of age ceremonies frequently have three key stages. First there is a *separation* of the individual from the state he or she is leaving behind. Frequently the initiates are taken to a place apart from the main village or settlement. Next follows the actual introduction to the new group that the person is joining – what has been called the stage of *transition* from one social state to the next. There is often some ordeal to be undergone and something to learn. Finally, there is often a ceremony of *reincorporation* of the person into society as a member of the new group.

The rituals practised by some Australian Aboriginal peoples show this pattern very clearly. In some tribes, for example, the young person undergoes a process of physical and mental weakening – a process that accords with the notion that the person is symbolically dying only to be reborn at the end of the ritual, as well as breaking links with their past life. This notion of death and rebirth is inherent in rites of passage in many cultures.

The next phase is educational. Becoming an adult involves being party to certain knowledge that has to be passed on. So the young person learns about the ancestor myths and the ceremonies and law of his people.

Finally, there is a ritual of bodily mutilation, such as the removal of a tooth, circumcision, or an incision in the penis, that identifies the individual with the new social grouping he has joined, bringing him back to society once more. This broad account could serve as a model for the initiation ceremonies of numerous Australian tribes. Similar ceremonies are also used by a still wider range of peoples all over the world.

Although the initiate is eventually brought back into society, the ritual may well have involved some permanent bodily marking. The initiate is thereby clearly differentiated from those who have not yet been through the coming-of-age ceremony.

Alternatively, it may have entailed a more superficial differentiation such as the initiate being allowed to wear different clothes from before, or to paint his or her body in a special way, or to go into some part of the village,

SORROWFUL STORY
Young boys perform a play about a group of children lost in a rainforest. The sad story mirrors the sadness over the loss of childhood felt by both initiates and their mothers.

such as a male or female clubhouse, that was out of bounds before.

The sequence of events that makes up the initiation ceremony of Gnau people of New Guinea shows how complex such rituals can be. Many of the stages of the ceremony are similar for boys and girls, although there are also important variations.

The day begins at dawn, when girls must go to wash with specially prepared scented water. The guests begin to assemble, and if a first child is to be initiated, matrilineal relatives will bring gifts. The men cook tubers which will be eaten mashed with coconut. The mother cooks a mixture of leaves and salt that the child eats. This releases the child from a number of

DRAMAS OF INITIATION, NEW GUINEA

Every five years or so each group of Gimi villages in New Guinea organizes a festival to initiate the sons of the community and to marry the daughters. This gathering of hundreds of people is punctuated by dramas performed by groups of people who call on the different houses and perform short plays. Sometimes as many as eight performances are given in a single night.

BOGEYMEN
Men rush around selecting initiates to terrify further. They are enacting the role of ancestor spirits showing the rules of good conduct to the young men.

FRIGHTENING SIGHTS
Older men force the initiates to stay isolated inside the men's circular house. Here, they are periodically frightened by the entrance of one of the men dressed in a terrifying mask. In addition, the young men are forced to spend long periods without food or sleep, and are made to sit for hours next to scorching fires.

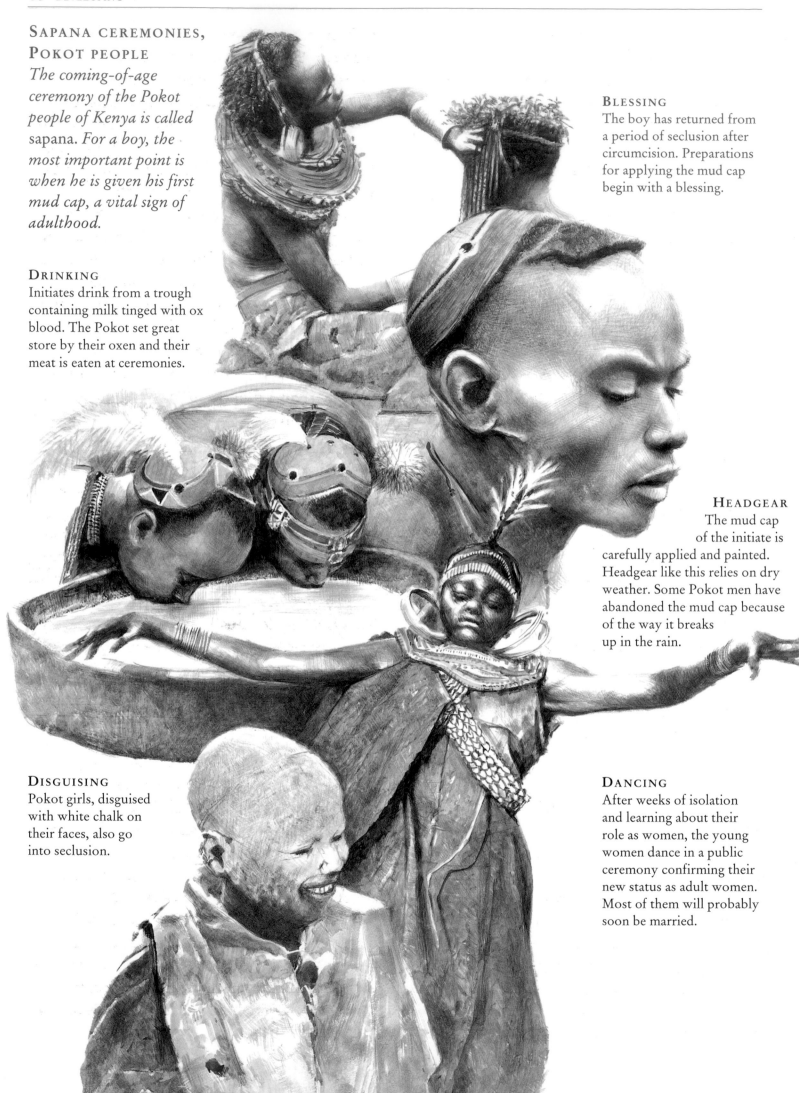

SAPANA CEREMONIES, POKOT PEOPLE

The coming-of-age ceremony of the Pokot people of Kenya is called sapana. *For a boy, the most important point is when he is given his first mud cap, a vital sign of adulthood.*

DRINKING
Initiates drink from a trough containing milk tinged with ox blood. The Pokot set great store by their oxen and their meat is eaten at ceremonies.

DISGUISING
Pokot girls, disguised with white chalk on their faces, also go into seclusion.

BLESSING
The boy has returned from a period of seclusion after circumcision. Preparations for applying the mud cap begin with a blessing.

HEADGEAR
The mud cap of the initiate is carefully applied and painted. Headgear like this relies on dry weather. Some Pokot men have abandoned the mud cap because of the way it breaks up in the rain.

DANCING
After weeks of isolation and learning about their role as women, the young women dance in a public ceremony confirming their new status as adult women. Most of them will probably soon be married.

prohibitions, including those against smoking and chewing betel.

Next, a headdress is put on the child. In the case of a boy, the first stage of this is done inside the men's house. Then the boy is taken away from the village to a secret place where a ceremony is performed that involves puncturing the boy's penis. Blood from a relative is also dripped over the boy and some of this blood is mixed with the stew of tubers and coconut.

In the next stage of the ceremony, the male relatives spit at the child with betel juice. For a girl, this is done in public, for a boy it is usually done in private. The red juice is then smeared with platters all over the child's body and allowed to dry.

The stew is now brought out in its traditional earthenware pot, and is eaten according to a ritual in which spells are recited. The meal is a highly significant part of the initiation. Children who are initiated together and eat the same stew thereby become ritual friend, a relationship that may be lifelong.

Finally the child's headdress is completed and shell ornaments are given. The proceedings end with a feast at which everyone eats and presentations of money are made to the child.

SEPARATE SPHERES

Many coming-of-age or initiation ceremonies happen in a place apart from the main settlement and the rituals are often performed in private. This can give such ceremonies an air of mystery, something that is rarely present in such public rites as weddings or naming ceremonies of infants.

There are different reasons for this seclusion. In rituals to mark the onset of menstruation, it is often to do with the fact that many peoples consider a woman impure or polluted in some way at this time. Either menstrual blood itself is seen as impure, or it is evidence that the woman is losing some of her pollution, which could be transmitted to any who come into contact with her during menstruation. Thus a young woman in Sri Lanka would expect to be isolated from the menfolk at the time of her first menses. As the anthropologist Deborah Winslow, who studied Buddhist, Catholic and Muslim families in the 1970s, reported, only two toddler brothers were left with a young menstruating Buddhist woman: 'All other males, including her father and grandfather, who lived in the house, were kept from seeing her. The *killa* (pollution), of first menstruation is said to be the strongest of all *killa* and particularly bad for men. Small boys are least vulnerable but it was still considered an unfortunate necessity that her two brothers had to be with her.' Catholic and Muslim women in Sri Lanka were also isolated at this stage in their lives, but the explanation generally given for this separation was that it was for their own protection rather than to shield men from pollution.

Where young men are coming of age, there are often secret ceremonies that embrace some of the ancient traditions of the people that need to be handed down to the next generation. This has led to the use of the rather confusing term 'secret society' to describe the groups of male initiates in places such as the Pacific Melanesian islands. In the West the term, 'secret society' seems to imply a group that meets in secret and whose membership is even secret. But while many of the rituals may be shrouded in secrecy, membership of the secret societies of the Pacific islands is far from mysterious and, indeed, may well embrace the entire adult male population.

Some of the best known of these societies are the *duk-duk* secret societies of the Bismarck Archipelago. The members, who wear masks over their heads and garments made of leaves, practise an initiation ceremony involving beating the novices. This and their other ceremonies take place in an enclosure in the forest, far away from the village.

ORDEAL AND CELEBRATION

Frequently at the heart of the ceremony is some painful physical ordeal – for example, some sort of surgical incision or circumcision, the making of cuts in the flesh to create scars (cicatrization), or the removal of part of a finger or a tooth.

However, the severity of the ordeal varies greatly from people to people. The !Kung, for example, have a ceremony for boys called *choma* when each boy's forehead is incised

CICATRIZATION
Among the Pokot people, young women are ritually scarred or cicatrized to mark their transition to adulthood. The scars are made on the stomach and sometimes on the back and waist area too.

with a vertical line. !Kung boys do not have to take part in *choma* and its importance is not so great as that of the first hunting kill.

The kill is marked with further ordeals. Cuts are made in various parts of the youth's body and medicinal herbs mixed with the fat of the hunted animal are rubbed into them. These actions are explained as helpful to the hunter (the herbs administered to the cuts in his arm make his aim better, those in the cuts in his brow make him see better, and so on). In addition, the kill is treated as something to be celebrated. The person after whom the young man is named usually gives him a spear.

For !Kung women also, coming of age is treated as a time for celebration. At the onset of her first menstrual period, the young woman is taken to a special shelter away from the camp. Here women and old men gather to sing special songs and perform a dance. The dance is performed by the women and two of the old men, who attach twigs to their heads to imitate the horns of the eland.

ORDEAL AND ANXIETY

The Muslim Hausa people of northwestern Nigeria and southern Niger place much pressure on initiates to observe their customs and ceremonies of coming of age correctly. For one thing, the sexes are segregated socially and, although schools are co-educational, young men have only male friends and young women keep female company. Great shame is attached to any Hausa woman who has had sexual experience before marriage.

The onset of menstruation is a time of particular anxiety for a young Hausa woman. She is told that she must in future keep away from men and is continuously watched by her mother. Indeed the anxiety to prevent inappropriate contact between adolescent girls and boys means that marriages are often arranged before the first menses. The menstruating woman must also adhere to many

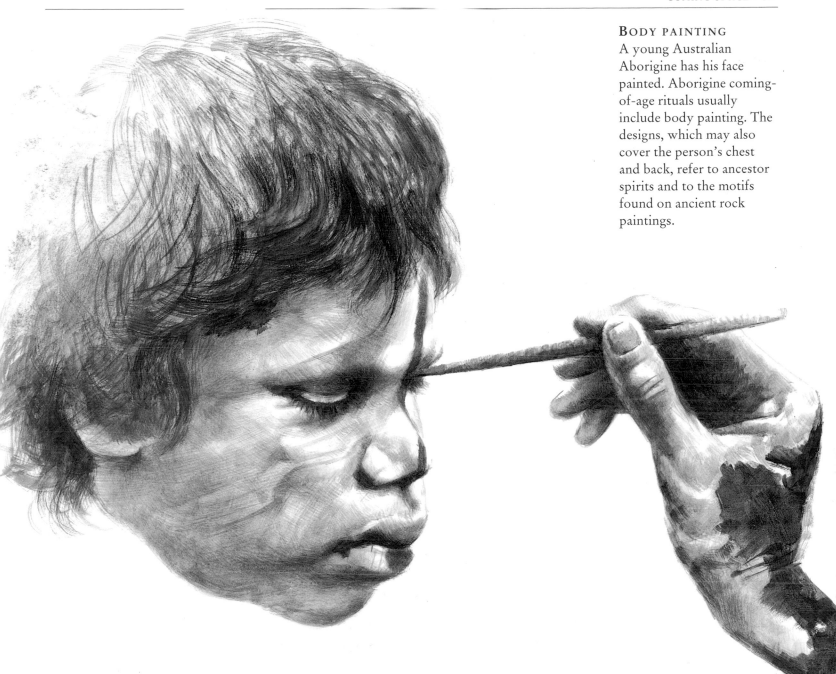

other restrictions. Not only must she refrain from sex with her husband, she must not pray, touch the Qur'an or fast during Ramadan. After menstruation, she must bathe, wash her hair, and cut her nails. Such restrictions apply whether it is her first period or her last.

LEARNING PROCESSES

Frequently it is not enough simply to go through a ceremony, even one involving a painful ordeal, in order to become an adult. There are traditions and laws to learn, and rules of conduct and further rituals to observe. So the formal passage from childhood to adulthood often involves a learning process in which the young person is taught about the ways of the adult world.

One notable example of this is in the ceremonies of the Pacific islands of Western and American Samoa. The culture of these islands was described by the anthropologist Margaret Mead in her book *Coming of Age in Samoa* (1928). Although many Samoans took issue with Mead's account of their culture, her observations were accurate in many respects – in particular, her descriptions of a highly structured society, with its complex rules of behaviour. Young men would learn many of these rules in the Aumaga, an organization of young men similar to that of the older men. Here the youngsters would learn 'to make speeches, to conduct themselves with gravity and decorum, to serve and drink the *kava* [a drink made from the aromatic roots of the kava shrub], to plan and execute group enterprises'. The young women of Samoa had their own equivalent of the Aumaga, called the Aualuma.

In other cultures, the learning process is more personal. When a Cheyenne youth killed a buffalo and presented it to the local shaman (priest or medicine man), for example, the shaman would bless both the boy and his family in accepting the carcass. The whole process would teach the boy not only about hunting, but also about rituals and the importance of the shaman in his society.

Religious instruction often forms the chief educational component of the initiation. This is familiar in Christian societies, where classes before confirmation prepare the initiate to become a full member of the church. Baptists

BEMP - A CELEBRATION OF THE KAYAPO PEOPLE OF BRAZIL

Sometimes a people create a festival that encompasses several of the traditional rites of passage, together perhaps with other rituals as well. The festival of Bemp, celebrated by the Kayapo Indians in Brazil, is such an event. This dry-season ritual is named after a local fish. As well as initiation rites, it includes the naming of children and marriage ceremonies.

SYMBOLISM
The striking headdresses are worn for an all-night vigil with a ceremonial partner. The radiating feathers symbolize the universe and the shaft stands for the rope on which the first Kayapo is believed to have descended from the sky.

HEADDRESSES
Men who take part in the initiation ceremony wear elaborate headdresses made of wax and feathers. The base of the headdress is shaped from beeswax.

use the ceremony of baptism in a similar way. Rather than baptizing infants, as is the usual Christian custom, they wait until the child or adult can make their own conscious decision to become part of the church. In other cultures the religious education prior to initiation is more wide-ranging. Hindu boys in India, for example, may be required to study their religion with a swami, who might teach subjects such as mathematics and literature as well as the sacred books. It was once traditional for every 13-year-old Jewish boy to give a scholarly address on Talmudic law at his Bar Mitzvah. Nowadays, it is more likely to be a speech or a prayer.

Nevertheless, the boy is likely to have undertaken a considerable amount of preparation for this occasion – in particular, to enable him to read the Torah, which he may now do in in the synagogue.

READY TO BE NAMED
A young participant in the festival is going to receive an ancestral name. Downy yellow parrot feathers are glued to his body and pale blue eggshells stuck to his head with latex.

BELONGING TO A GROUP

As we have seen, initiation into adulthood frequently entails becoming part of a special group within society. In places such as Australia, Melanesia and North America, this involves becoming part of a totem group – a group with a common mythical (and often animal) ancestor, concerned with passing on information about that ancestor and with ancestor-worship generally.

In addition to totem groups, there are other groups, sometimes referred to as fraternities, which also have a religious basis, but that may exist independently of totem groups or be intertwined with them.

An example of such an initiation ceremony comes from the Zuñi of New Mexico. It is the rite of initiation into the Ko'tikili, a society that includes all adult men of the tribe. The child's sponsor (ideally the husband, eldest son or eldest brother of the midwife who attended at the child's birth) leads him into his ceremonial house or *kiva*. Two women place folded rugs on his back and the sponsor wraps the initiate's head in a cloth so that he cannot see. Then men wearing the masks of Sayathlia gods beat the child four times on the back with branches of yucca. The women are also struck, and the young man is struck again. Next, the cloth is removed from his head and an eagle's feather is attached to his hair by the sponsor. The four 'gods' take off their masks and are recognized as men. The child and three fellow initiates then come before the 'gods'. A 'god' gives each one of them a mask and a yucca branch, and the initiates belabour the 'gods'. Finally, the 'gods' are given back their masks and branches, with which they once again beat the sponsors.

Other North American tribes, such as the Navaho, use similar rituals, and there are also similarities with Australian ceremonies. In both cultures the sacred objects (masks in North America, bull-roarers in Australia) are

APACHE COMING OF AGE

In this ceremony, a young Apache woman follows a coming-of-age ritual that brings her close to a revered ancestor spirit. In particular, the dances are designed to attract benevolent spirits, while allowing her to escape from evil forces.

SPONSORSHIP

A key figure in the ceremony is the sponsor, who assists at the ceremony and has a special relationship with the initiate. The young woman's father presents a feather to the sponsor, who in accepting the feather accepts this role.

DANCING

The initiate dances while kneeling on a pad of buckskin. She is directed by her father, who holds her sacred cane, and her sponsor, holding an eagle feather in each hand.

RUNNING

The young woman runs around her sacred cane. She must go fast so that no evil person can catch her.

YELLOW SHOWER

Bright yellow cattail pollen, a substance that is considered holy by the Apache, is sprinkled over the young woman.

THE FINAL DANCE

In the later stages of the ceremony, the initiate is painted all over and blessed in turn from four sides. Then she takes part in a dance around the frame of a tepee.

shown to the initiates, who are permitted to use them without danger from the spirits. The initiate is thus gradually made familiar with the instruments of the supernatural, without the fear of coming to harm.

Another common way of distinguishing initiates is, literally, to mark them using body paint. African ceremonies have a particularly rich repertoire of symbolic colours.

DYING AND BEING BORN AGAIN

The transition from one stage of life to another is considered such a major step that, in many cultures, symbolic death forms a significant part of a ritual in which rebirth occurs when the initiate is ready to be reintroduced to the community. Such a concept is familiar in some African cultures, where the initiate is considered dead in relation to his past life. It is also encountered in the coming-of-age ceremonies of the North American Ojibway people. Here, the men who preside over the ritual symbolically 'kill' all the participants and 'resurrect' them again at the end of each stage in the ceremony.

Even where the idea of death is not mentioned specifically, there is often a stage where the initiate acts as if dead, in the sense that he or she is rendered totally passive. The individual sometimes even goes into a trance, as do those being initiated into the Brazilian Candomblé religion. Such effects are brought on in a variety of ways in different cultures – for example, with drugs or by exhaustion or isolation. The implication of the ritual is, however, similar: an old life is being left behind and a new one is being begun.

Initiation rituals of all types have the effect of keeping the stages of life separate, emphasizing the distinction between child and adult. An elaborate ceremony may be a way of showing the importance of traditional knowledge or lore, reinforcing the power of the adult group. Or it may simply serve to clarify the individual's place in society. In both cases the essential difference between the childhood and adult states is being stressed.

MODERN PRESSURES, NEW RITUALS

In the secular society of the industrialized West, some traditional coming-of-age rites are less commonly observed than in the past. But even though one reason for such ceremonies is to ease the passage from childhood to adulthood, it cannot be said that the decline in such formal rituals is because this passage has become any easier in the developed world. Indeed, the pressures on the western adolescent – whether from school or media, parents or peers – are just as great as they ever were and there are numerous modern rituals that help to fill the gap that has been left. Some are almost as much a part of the establishment as the old religious rituals.

Take the degree ceremony. Every college and university has some form of gathering at which the year's successful candidates are

TIES THAT BIND
Members and former members of many British male social groups (such as military regiments and public schools) wear a mark of belonging in the form of a special tie. The right to wear such a tie indicates membership of an exclusive and often privileged part of adult society.

1 Oxford University
2 Royal Scots Guards
3 Royal Gloucester Hussars
4 Old Etonians
5 Old Rugbyians
6 All England Lawn Tennis Club
7 Edinburgh University
8 Royal Marines

1

formally awarded their degrees and sent away from the world of education and into the world of work. Some degree ceremonies have a high level of ritual content. Most involve speeches and the wearing of academic gowns (the design and trimmings of the latter reflecting the university hierarchy). Some, like that at the University of Oxford, involve formal processions, and the reading of a discourse in Latin.

In a similar fashion, there are new versions of the formal entry of the debutante into society. The traditional upper-class English version of this, at which young women embark on a season of parties, in search (in theory, at least) of a marriage partner, has inspired imitations and can be compared to like rituals in other places.

Even the very different American social system followed suit with formal balls and cotillions for the well-to-do young at the turn of the century. But a more widespread American tradition is the high-school prom. Young people don unfamiliar formal clothes (ball gowns and tuxedos) and attend their first all-night party – or at least, the first that receives adult approval. The evening dress, the licence to stay out all night, even the arrival in a limousine, all represent introductions to the adult world.

But modern coming-of age-ceremonies are not always as decorous as this. While the well-to-do have their proms and degree ceremonies, the society of the street has rougher, but no less necessary, initiation rituals. To gain entry into a gang, a young initiate might have to fight some of the established members, or commit a robbery and share the proceeds with his new companions, or might simply don the distinctive 'uniform' of the group. Street youths in Rio de Janeiro have to ride on top of electric trains, risking death if they touch the overhead wires.

New coming-of-age rituals are constantly being invented to reflect the realities of the societies in which people live, even enrolling modern technology in the rite of passage into the risky and challenging adult world.

2   3   4   5   6   7   8

Marriage

The novel *The Jungle* by the American writer
Upton Sinclair, is set amongst the immigrant
workers of Chicago and begins with a
wedding. The ceremony has just finished and
the Lithuanian family and their friends, who
are the main characters of the book, are
celebrating. There is a great feast, accompanied
by speeches and music. Everyone can eat as
much as they want, for it is the first principle
of the feast that none should go hungry. And
then there is dancing – two-steps, folk dances
from Lithuania, wild abandoned dances that
the dancers make up as they move, and finally
the *acziavimas*, a ceremony three or four hours
long involving one uninterrupted dance.

As we read, we realise how much this
celebration means to those who take part. For
the older people, many in national costume, it
is as if they are once more back in the old
country, a land that for the most part can only
be a dim and distant memory. For the younger
ones, it is a chance – a very rare chance – to
take part in an activity that is pure pleasure,
and to eat a decent meal. These are poor people
who are so oppressed by the drudgery of their
lives that many of them simply forget this
holiday that meant so much at home. But, even
though they have no money to pay for it, they
hang on to their wedding celebration as the
sole remaining symbol of their cultural
identity, and as a rare opportunity for spiritual
and physical nourishment.

A KEY TURNING POINT

All societies celebrate some form of marriage,
and many afford such celebration the
importance it is given by the Lithuanian
immigrants in *The Jungle*. Marriage is one of
the great rites of passage, signalling as it does

MARRIAGE AS CELEBRATION
From the solemnity of the marriage
vows, to the celebration of the
dance, weddings are some of the
longest and most elaborate of rituals.

the key turning-point in the vast majority of adult lives.

There are many examples of how this importance is revealed by wedding ceremonies around the world. The ancient Romans placed laurel wreaths, symbolic of victory, on the heads of the newly married couple. At traditional wedding ceremonies in Russia and some of the Baltic states, the bride and groom are crowned like royalty. In the Malay Peninsula, there is also the notion that the couple are 'king and queen for a day' when they are married. And in most societies the wedding celebration, which centres on the bridal couple and their relationship, is designed to make them feel special.

This sense of the importance of the occasion is not surprising, for much is at stake at a wedding. What happens on that day will influence two people – not to mention their children – for the rest of their lives. It will have repercussions for their families, perhaps instigating new friendships and alliances, and cementing old ties.

What is more, weddings and the way they are conducted often reflect the structure of society as a whole. Observance of the rules about whom one may marry can perhaps be

MARRIAGE TO THE GODS
The idea of a symbolic marriage to the deity appears in many societies. In the Christian West, the idea of the nun as 'bride of Christ' is familiar. In India, girls are sometimes given the spiritual blessing accorded by a symbolic marriage to one of the Hindu gods. Unlike the western nun, however, the young Hindu woman may undergo a conventional marriage later in life.

interpreted as an affirmation of the social order by the couple.

In contrast to the apprehension or pain of the coming-of-age rite and the grief of the funeral, wedding ceremonies are designed to be enjoyable for the participants. There may be tears, it is true – tears for the loss of a relative to a new family or clan, for example – but the emphasis is on celebration and merry-making – with eating, dancing, music, and other entertainments. People may travel great distances to join in, so it is also a chance to renew acquaintance with old friends and distant relatives: a true celebration.

Psychological effects

The purpose of the wedding ceremony is not simply to celebrate this crucial stage in a couple's life and make it public, though it certainly does this. It also has an important psychological function: it helps the couple to prepare for a major change in their lives.

This is done in a number of ways. Sometimes the preparation for marriage includes actual instruction about how a married couple should behave – this may involve serious ethical teaching or less formal advice, perhaps from an older relative. In some

Mixing cultures

Nowadays, many wedding ceremonies show a mixture of cultural influences. For example, where one religion has replaced another as the orthodoxy, the prevailing ceremony may retain elements of the former religion. Such a mixture of influences may also be seen in secular wedding ceremonies in which religious elements are sometimes retained, perhaps for reasons of nostalgia.

Eastern and western dress

At different points in the ceremony a bride at an elaborate Japanese wedding may wear a traditional kimono and a western-style white dress.

Hindu and Islam

A couple in Malaysia will be married under Islamic law with a Muslim ceremony. But their country was once Hindu, and Hindu traditions – for example, that of treating the couple like royalty on their wedding day – may still also be observed.

societies, magical rites that are believed to be vital for the success of the marriage are performed. In other cultures, satisfactory negotiation of the business side of the marriage – dowry or bride-price, for example – cements the bond between the two families, giving support to the couple.

The main focus of the ceremony is sometimes legal, providing a contract that sets out the rights and duties of the couple and providing proof that they have married. Sometimes the main thrust of the ceremony is religious. Frequently there is a mixture of both these elements, or even two separate ceremonies. In France, for example, a couple must be legally married by the local official at the Town Hall. They can then choose to have a religious ceremony in addition.

Different societies have different priorities and stress these themes in varying ways. But some functions are common to marriage ceremonies in many cultures. For example, like other rites of passage, the wedding is designed to allay the stress that accompanies change by making the transition enjoyable. The wedding also proclaims the new social status of the two people involved and encourages the rest of society to recognize this and to support them in their new roles.

Arranging a marriage

In the West and in places where a 'westernized' lifestyle prevails, people expect to choose their own marriage partners. People brought up in such cultures find it difficult to imagine allowing someone else to make a choice that will affect their future life and happiness. But for most of the world, and throughout most of human history until recent times, this has not been the case. For many people, marriage is a matter arranged by parents, who find a partner for their child, taking into consideration established guidelines concerning the class and wealth of a prospective partner, his or her

relationship to the other partner, and so on. In some places, a professional matchmaker is called in to help in the selection of a marriage partner. While this may take the proceedings yet another step away from the people who will become the main participants, such an intermediary can bring experience and contacts that the individuals and family alone would not be able to provide.

Arranged marriages are becoming less common as more and more countries assume western customs. They used to be the norm in Japan, for example, where a go-between would be employed and the lengthy pre-nuptial negotiations would be conducted around a formal meeting table. The proceedings would include a ceremony called *mi ai*, or mutual seeing, in which the two young people were introduced, giving them the chance to observe each other. If the parties were satisfied with each other, the wedding negotiations would proceed with speed. Otherwise the go-between would be told to look for another partner. However, the westernization of Japan has led to a decline in the number of marriages arranged in this way.

Arranged marriages are also common in Arab countries such as Saudi Arabia, where the alliance between the families is considered as important as the feelings of the couple. A marriage between cousins is particularly prized because it is seen to enrich the extended family rather than diluting it by links with outsiders. However, the woman has to give her final approval for the choice of husband.

In some places, the marriage negotiations begin during the childhood of one or both partners. This was the tradition in many of the Pacific Melanesian islands, such as Vanuatu. Here, it was normal for girls of seven or eight to be betrothed to a 20-year-old man. In New Britain, a youth of about 14 years old would be betrothed to a girl of about eight. Those who were betrothed at such a young age would often be sent to the home of their prospective

THE MEANING OF FEASTING

Food and feasting is a vital part of many wedding ceremonies as this artistic play on Bruegel's Wedding Feast *depicts. The joining together by those close to the bridal couple in celebration can be seen as an extension of the union to the larger community. The food can also be a gift and a means of showing hospitality – one family often provides the wedding feast. And it can offer a welcome diversion for the couple before they rejoin society.*

STUFF OF LIFE

In the Ukraine – an area famous for its agriculture, especially wheat-growing – it is fitting that elaborately decorated bread should form part of the wedding meal. The couple are thereby reminded of the chief source of their future livelihood.

ARCHITECTURAL MASTERPIECE

The traditional white-iced, multi-tiered wedding cake, said by some to be derived from the design of the spire of St Bride's Church in London, is the centrepiece of most British wedding feasts. The couple are supposed to cut the cake by holding the knife together – an action that symbolizes fertility as well as hospitality.

TOGETHERNESS

A Javanese couple eat food from each other's plates – a gesture that symbolizes the sharing of resources that marriage requires. Mixing of yellow and white rice also forms part of the Javanese ceremony.

LARGESSE

Even amongst the poor, it is important to put on as rich a display of food as possible and so to demonstrate the traditional virtue of hospitality. Here a Romanian couple have laid out the food all over the floor and furniture.

DRESSING TO GET MARRIED

Couples in many cultures wear special costumes for the wedding ceremony. These garments make the bride and groom stand out from the crowd. The traditional costume may also have symbolic significance, like the western bride's white dress. In some cultures, there are also special clothes for courtship rituals.

YEMEN
The face of a Yemeni bride is decorated in a ceremony involving the women of both families. Long elaborate earrings represent prosperity, while woollen braids are an expression of strength and fertility.

MEXICO
At a country wedding in Mexico, the bride is shrouded in a thick white veil until halfway through the ceremony. Rosaries and crucifixes – heirlooms of both the families – adorn her costume and the groom's white robe.

KAZAKHSTAN
In Kazakhstan the conical hat is a celebratory symbol worn not just at weddings but also at other festivals and celebrations.

MOROCCO

A royal bride in Marrakech is bedecked in layers of robes and headdresses in a ritual that lasts several hours. Her costume makes movement difficult, and she must sit on a cushion for the entire three-hour marriage ceremony.

ECUADOR

In Ecuador the groom holds a candle that burns throughout the ceremony. Its constant flame represents eternal love.

NIGER

A Fulani man from Niger paints his face and adorns his hair with ropes of beads and shells for the festival of Geerewol, at which he hopes to attract a wife.

JAPAN

At this Japanese wedding, dress is traditional, the bride in a kimono and characteristic headdress.

WESTERN EUROPE

The traditional European wedding costume – the bride's white dress, symbolic of purity, and the groom's formal suit – is well known, even though it has only been used widely since the last century. It is imitated in places as far away from Europe as Japan. In the United States, this form of dress is still popular, although nowadays the bride often dispenses with the traditional veil, and may choose pastel shades instead of white for her gown.

partner, to give them a chance to get to know each other before the marriage.

CHOOSING YOUR OWN PARTNER

In contrast to the practice in New Britain, women of wealthy families in New Caledonia were allowed some say in the choice of partner. Suitors would arrive at the young woman's village and stand in a row. In front of them would be a leaf on which pieces of coconut were placed. Each man picked up a piece of coconut, bit off a piece and laid it back on the leaf. The young woman would then pick up

BERBER FESTIVAL OF BRIDES

In Morocco many people preserve customs that prevailed before the country embraced Islam. The most famous of the ceremonies of the Ait Hadiddou people of the Atlas Mountains is the Festival of Brides, which takes place every September. In a matter of days, couples progress from first meeting to marriage. And the speed with which such marriages are arranged is paralleled by the ease of divorce. Indeed many of the men and women at the festival are there to look for new partners after divorce.

and eat the piece bitten off by the man of her choice. The man would then pay the required bride-price to her relatives and depart with her. The woman could remain single if she favoured none of the suitors. Many similar ceremonies of partner-choice have been recorded in various parts of the world.

In Madagascar there is a ritual in which the roles are reversed. The woman, who has been selected by an intermediary as a partner for a particular husband, has to stand in a group with other young women, so that the prospective husband can make his choice. The ceremony is known as 'being compared'.

ARRIVALS

Thousands come to the festival and the occasion provides the chance to trade in the produce of the land as well as to arrange marriages. Prospective husbands can be identified by their white garments – especially the white turban with a square of cloth hanging down behind.

PREPARATIONS

The women wear a veil and headdress. The latter, often decorated with silver discs and glass beads, hides most of the carefully made up face. A woollen cape ensures that would-be husbands can see little of their prospective brides. Widows and divorced women wear special pointed headdresses.

Dancing – from the formal displays of traditional societies to the modern western disco – often provides a forum in which partners can be chosen. Dance allows a variety of approaches: one can be close or distant, one can stress intimacy or sheer display, one can be subtle or provocative. Indeed, it is possible to combine these contraries in such a way as to give expression to erotic feelings without being excessively invasive or forward.

Often the sexual content of the dance is attributed to some animal. In the *schuhplattler* or slap-shoe dance of Bavaria, for example, the man imitates the mating dance of the mountain cock. His clicks, hissings, foot-stampings and hand-clappings are all reminiscent of the bird.

A less frenzied example is a dance of the young Watusi women of Zaire. They imitate the slow, stately progress of the mountain crane, as they advance, retreat and turn, their outstretched arms waving slowly like wings. One bare-breasted girl will stroke the cheek of another girl in a movement that symbolizes the transfer of the charm of fertility.

An equally elegant display is put on by the young men of the Wodaabe people of Niger. The men of one clan make up their faces elaborately, don flowing robes, and sing and

WAITING GAMES
Groups of men and women watch members of the opposite sex while they stand and chat. The women's clothing gives them the opportunity to look at the men without really being seen themselves.

ENCOUNTERS
Encouraged by their relatives and friends, men and women gradually begin to talk to each other and to pair off. If the couple agree to become betrothed, they go to an official scribe, who writes them a marriage application in Arabic.

MORE WAITING
Their written applications prepared, the couples lines up outside the tent of the *qadi*, an official of the Minister of Justice.

OFFICIALLY MARRIED
Provided the application is in order, the couple's marriage is

endorsed. The groom pays a fee to the government and gives his wife 50 dihrams: they are officially married. A divorced or widowed woman accompanies her husband back to his village. A first-time bride returns to her own village and joins her husband later in the year.

WEDDING, RURAL BURGUNDY

France is a modern industrialized republic that is also rich in ancient Catholic traditions. It is therefore appropriate that French weddings should contain both traditional and modern, sacred and secular, elements. It is common for French couples to have two wedding ceremonies, one secular, one religious (although only the first is a legal requirement), and for traditional customs to be mixed in with the attendant revelry. This example is taken from Burgundy, but other regions of France could supply similar ceremonies and customs.

BEFORE THE TRICOLOR
The wedding party assembles at the Town Hall for the civil ceremony, presided over by the mayor, against the background of the French tricolor.

PROCESSION
The bride, groom, and their parents lead the wedding party in a procession from civil to religious ceremony. It makes the wedding a very public affair. Nowadays, the procession is often in cars, with horns blowing.

BEFORE GOD
In church the couple exchange vows, the congregation prays and sings hymns, and the priest gives an address. The couple are now married in the eyes of the church.

CONGRATULATIONS
The guests gather outside the church and congratulate the couple. After this, everyone goes to a public hall for the vin d'honneur, a drinks party at which the whole community (not just the wedding guests) give their best wishes to the couple.

FEAST
After another procession, the guests arrive at the home of the bride's or groom's parents for a lavish feast, featuring local produce. After speeches and toasts, the couple lead the guests in a dance.

COUPLE-HUNTING
The couple leave the feast in the early hours of the morning, while the celebrations are still in full swing. According to local custom, they go and hide somewhere in or near the town. A group of young friends are then given the task of finding them. When they are found, the couple are made to drink a repulsive concoction from a chamber pot. This done, they are left in peace. The feasting resumes the following lunchtime and they are expected to be there.

dance as a group in graceful anticlockwise movements. The women of other clans gather around in a circle to appraise the dancers. Eye contact between one of the dancers and one of the watchers may be enough to start their courtship. Eyes are important to the Wodaabe, and in another ritual to attract a partner, the men will roll their heavily made-up eyes.

Once the choice of partner has been made, many cultures observe preliminary rituals before the wedding itself. Often there is a formal request by the man for the 'hand' of the woman. Usually the man's approach to the relatives of his intended is respectful and formal, but there are exceptions. In Finland it used to be the custom for the man to arrive at the home of his chosen woman's family, firing his rifle.

Where there is no formal request to the woman's family, there are generally direct approaches to the prospective partner, with exchanges of gifts and visits. The gifts may be anything from betel nuts or tobacco, traditional in Borneo, to the flowers or jewellery, commonly given to women by their suitors in western societies. After these tentative exchanges, there is a often a period of engagement in which the couple get to know each other better before making the final commitment to marriage itself. In Europe and America the engagement may be formally marked by the gift of a ring from the man to the woman. There may also be an engagement party in which relatives and friends bring gifts.

SIMPLE OR COMPLEX?

Marriage occurs everywhere, but there are marked differences between wedding ceremonies around the world, not just in what happens, but in the degree of complexity. Why should this be?

One reason is the relative importance placed on marriage by society, which in turn depends on the way that society is organized. Some societies are organized around descent through the female line (these are known as matrilineal societies); others have descent through the male line (patrilineal societies). In a matrilineal society there are groups of male and female relatives united by the female line. The brothers and other male relatives of a woman provide economic support for her and her children, and share in the upbringing of the children, too. The father of the children, on the other hand, belongs to a different social group and may visit his wife only at night. He will in turn provide for the children of his sisters and other female relatives.

In such a situation, the bonds between husband and wife, father and children, are likely to be less tight than in a patrilineal society. Here, the father traditionally takes part in the upbringing of the children – from both social and economic points of view – and the mother is generally dependent on her husband for economic support.

It is not surprising, therefore, that the institution of marriage is given more emphasis in patrilineal than in matrilineal societies, and that marriage ceremonies in the former are generally longer and more elaborate and often involve the transfer of property from one family to another. In addition, where the ties of marriage form such as important aspect of the structure of society, there is likely to be great encouragement for marriages to be long-lasting and this encouragement can be built into the marriage ceremony.

INDIVIDUAL RITUALS

Most forms of wedding ceremony involve some form of ritual aimed directly at the couple themselves. They may be asked questions, which range in content from enquiries about their prowess and fitness for the roles of husband and wife to promises to remain faithful to the new partner. This is essentially the private part of the ceremony, but it usually takes place in front of witnesses.

In many marriage ceremonies a ring is given. It can act as a token of the promise between the two partners to be faithful to each other, and as a confirmation that property has been exchanged between the two families. It is also a fertility symbol, and ring-shaped tokens (wreaths and garlands as well as finger-rings) have been a part of the wedding ceremony in many cultures for thousands of years.

RITUAL MEETINGS

Weddings often represent a gathering of the community on a large scale. In societies where there is little travel and where the bride, groom and their families live near to each other, the whole town or village may turn out with the intention of having a good time. In cases where the couple come from places far apart, the wedding may seem even more like a vast family meeting, with people staying overnight, meeting old friends and making new ones.

So weddings often include rituals that make it possible for everyone to meet everyone else, either formally or informally. This is one of the functions of the wedding feast – bringing together the families and friends of both partners and breaking the ice. But there are also more formal devices. European and American weddings, for example, often have reception lines, during which the guests formally greet the couple and their parents.

Many other common components of a wedding celebration, from dancing to gift-giving, can be used as a means of bringing the guests together. And so all these strategies fulfil the dual role of making everyone feel at home and reinforcing social continuity.

PROCESSIONS

Such ritual meetings remind us that marriage ceremonies are often highly public affairs. Dancing and feasting help to make this the

ROYAL WEDDING, SOUTHERN AFRICA
In 1977 a princess from Swaziland married the king of the Zulu people of South Africa. As one might expect, the wedding was conducted with great ceremony. In addition to loud music and vigorous dancing, the celebrations featured lavish costumes, a mock-battle, and gift-giving by both the bride's and the groom's family. Many of the rituals emphasized the coming together of two peoples who had been enemies in the 19th century.

case, but even more so does the procession. From India to Slovakia, weddings frequently involve processions through the streets. The overt purpose of the procession varies from culture to culture. It might be a way of getting the whole wedding party from one place to another; it might signal the arrival of the bride and her attendants; the bride and groom may even have separate processions.

All this marching around has a number of important benefits. First, everyone, even those members of the community who do not come

FAREWELLS

The princess is given a send-off by friends and kinswomen in Swaziland. She bids formal farewell to her relatives, dancing with her attendants, her breasts bared to show her humiliy. Her family sit and watch. The sleeping mat and gourd in front of the dancers symbolize the household she is moving. She holds a knife and two traditional spears called *assegais* to show that she is going to join another clan. The ox's gall bladder tied to her head is a token of good fortune.

A PRINCESS PREPARES

After a ritual bathing, the bride is annointed with ox-gall. She is then dressed for the wedding itself.

WAR AND PEACE

Swazi warrors engage in a mock battle with their Zulu hosts in the royal enclosure. This is a reminder of the times when the two peoples were truly at war. It also paves the way for the bride, who sweeps into the kraal in the wake of the warriors.

THE PRINCESS APPEARS

She is arrayed in her headdress of feathers and she carries a sword: both are signs of her royal blood. Dancers and musicians surround her. She and the groom, who wears a cloak of leopardskin and a necklace of lion claws, take their vows.

DANCING AND GIFT-GIVING

The entire assembly dances to celebrate the union. The bride's father has already given his cattle to the Zulu king. Now it is the princess's turn to honour her new in-laws with presents. Dozens of relatives of the groom sit in wait for gifts of sleeping mats, blankets and bowls. Again, the princess bares her breasts in humility.

to the actual ceremony, can look on, and so the event is given instant publicity. Secondly, the man and woman are once again seen in the context of the whole community, and are further prepared for their reintegration into society as a couple. Thirdly, the community itself is prepared for this coming-together.

The public nature of the procession may also serve to emphasize the legality of the marriage. This is not simply a matter of obeying society's rules about the choice of a partner. There may also be the need to show that the correct dowry or bride-price has been paid. On the Pacific islands of Melanesia, for example, a bride might process with the shells, necklaces, feathers and other ornaments and valuables that have been paid as her price. It was traditional to string these items from poles and carry them high for all to see.

The North African ceremony of the bride box was an effective way of making a union public. The woman was put into a wooden cage and paraded through the streets to the man's home. A sizeable group of followers, including musicians, attendants, and interested friends and neighbours accompanied her in the procession, which usually took place by moonlight. Others would shout their good wishes from doorways. On arrival at the man's house, the bride would be released from her box, which would then be decorated with flowers, jewellery and presents. There followed a two-day honeymoon period, during which the couple were left in peace. After this time the box was placed on the roof of the house for all to see, as a sign that the couple were now ready to receive visits from their friends and family.

DANCING

The dance is one of the most common features of wedding celebrations around the world. It can take many forms, from the non-stop whirlwind dance at the Lithuanian wedding described at the beginning of this chapter to the highly ritualized mock battle in the Zulu-Swazi wedding described on pages 84-5. As can be seen from this variety, dances during wedding ceremonies have many different purposes.

Dances may be instructional, acting out the role of ideal husband or ideal wife. Or there may be an elegant solo dance, such as that danced by the bride at a traditional Bajau (water-gypsy) wedding in the Philippines. But more often than not, both partners are likely to take part. It is not uncommon in the West, for example, for the bridal couple to start the dancing on their own at their wedding, with the guests joining in later. Such an action neatly combines two reasons for the dance – it celebrates the new union and it confirms that the couple will rejoin society and become part of a harmonious whole.

MAKING MISCHIEF

Wedding ceremonies, which are to a large extent about absorbing a change to the social order, can include more than their fair share of riotous

behaviour. It is not simply that the participants are having a good time – although the mixture of youth, alcohol and high spirits certainly accounts for some of it. But any rite of passage is, almost by definition, happening at a time of potential difficulty. Modern doctors tell us that any major life change is a potential cause of stress. At times like this, old rivalries are perhaps just as likely to be remembered as new ties. Sometimes adversaries, who normally avoid contact with each other, are obliged to come to the ceremony, creating anxiety for all.

Ritual horseplay can be a way of diffusing these potential tensions. It can also offer a normally reticent (or even repressed) portion of society the chance to express themselves. A good example is a custom sometimes seen in rural weddings in India. The reticent section of society here is made up of the women, who normally accept the rules of purdah. But at a wedding the kinswomen of the bride are sometimes to be found ritually abusing the male relatives of the groom, smearing them with foul-looking pastes or with scarlet or indigo dye. Such uncharacteristic actions probably help release the tensions that can build up between in-laws, as well as acting as a brief holiday from purdah for the women.

Another example is the ritual of 'sham capture' of the bride, a ritual that once took place in several societies, notably on the islands of the Torres Straits between Australia and Papua New Guinea. This is the mock abduction of the bride by the groom and a group of his kin. The ritual takes place where all the marriage arrangements have been agreed to everyone's satisfaction – it does not represent a serious attempt to kidnap the bride or to use her as some sort of negotiating tool. Sham capture normally occurs in places where marriage represents the union of two separate groups of kin, not simply of two individuals. Like the Indian women's use of their dyes, sham capture is a way of diffusing any tensions that might exist between the two groups.

MONEY AND MARRIAGE

In many cultures marriage is as much a financial as an emotional event. Often the 'marriagability' of a woman is related to her parents' ability to provide a suitably lavish dowry for the family of the groom. Alternatively, it may be the fact that the man's family can afford the relevant bride-price that enables the ceremony to go ahead. Such financial arrangements help to cement family ties in many societies.

SYMBOL OF VALUE
The Surma women of Ethiopia stretch their lower lips by inserting wooden or earthenware plates. Gradually larger and larger plates are inserted so that, over a period of years, considerable extension is achieved. By tradition, the larger the lip extension, the larger the bride-price that the woman can command.

In other cultures, 'holidays' from the normal rules of behaviour may be taken separately by the bride and groom. Pre-wedding parties for the bride and female friends or groom and male friends are common in western societies. Such 'stag nights' and 'hen nights' offer the chance for both partners to have a last fling before entering the more restrictive regime of marriage. Sometimes there seems to be a symbolic attempt to sabotage the marriage on stag nights – by playing practical jokes on the groom, or by plying him with so much alcohol that he will be unable to turn up at the ceremony on the following day. Such customs have been seen by some commentators as last-ditch attempts to prevent the groom from leaving the society of his single male friends.

MONEY AND MARRIAGE
The alliance between two people, and therefore between their families or clans, is also often a financial arrangement. This phenomenon goes back to ancient times. In Babylonian law, for example, it was laid down that a wife should bring property with her, thereby making a material contribution to supporting the new family. The custom can take various forms and is especially common in patrilineal societies, where marriage is often seen as an exchange of women between strongly male-dominated kinship groups. A woman in such societies will often be expected to bring some of her inheritance to her husband's kinship group. This payment is known as a dowry. Traditionally, especially in places where wealth was measured in terms of farm land, the dowry was in land. Nowadays, where the custom survives, it is usually a money payment. The tradition of the dowry was once widespread throughout Europe and continued until recently in many Mediterranean and southern Asian cultures.

The other widespread type of marriage payment is bride-price (sometimes known as bridewealth). This is paid by the husband's family to that of the bride, and is intended to compensate her family for the loss of her labour. The custom of the purchase of a bride in this way goes back far into history and is

HINDU WEDDING, RURAL CENTRAL INDIA

Hinduism is a religion with many variations: beliefs and practises vary in different places. There is also an elaborate caste system, based on four broad groups of castes, each with its own customs. Hindus practise some of the most lengthy and elaborate rites of passage, although some of the ceremonies are now less complex than they were.

THE WEDDING PROCESSIONS

During the days leading up to the wedding ceremony there is at least one procession. The groom travels to the bride's house, where he is received as an honoured guest. He is accompanied by a large party and also by musicians. Some of the people walk, but the groom and close relatives travel on specially decorated bullock carts. Gifts are exchanged, and amongst higher castes the bride's relatives may present large sums of money to the family of the groom.

MAKING THE ARRANGEMENTS

Astrology has an important part to play in traditional Hinduism, and the local astrologer is likely to be consulted about both the choice of partner and the date of the wedding.

THE BRIDE'S PREPARATIONS

The bride dresses and applies make-up for the ceremony, a process that may take several hours. She wears special clothes and jewellery. Her female relatives decorate her skin with red dye.

still common today in certain traditional African societies.

Although the traditions of dowry and bride-price evolved as a way of ensuring the stability of kinship-groups, such payments can cause social problems, too. In 1901, for example, the ruling classes of the Solomon Islands met to discuss the levels of bride-price. It seemed that the amounts of money demanded had become so high that only the rich could afford to marry. Bride-price rates were therefore fixed at a more reasonable level – with a special higher rate payable if the families of both partners were chiefs.

In other areas, the difficulty of paying the bride-price or dowry has been solved by introducing a system of payment by instalments.

Nowadays, the dowry system has been rejected in many places, even though it may have been beneficial for kinship groups as a whole. In India, for example, there were cases of women being maltreated and even murdered when dowry payments were not met in full. This led to the legal abolition of the dowry system in the 1960s, although it is still practised in some areas.

ALTERNATIVES TO MARRIAGE

Nowadays, particularly in secular societies, many couples decide to live together without

THE WEDDING CEREMONY

The ceremony itself is held outdoors, either in a specially erected marriage booth or in a courtyard of the bride's house. A fire is lit in a metal container. Sanskrit verses are recited and the couple throw rice into the fire. The bride's sari and the groom's long shirt are then knotted together. The groom takes the bride by the hand and leads her seven times around the fire. The number seven symbolizes the irrevocable nature of the union. After the ceremony there is a feast with professional dancers.

THE JOURNEY HOME

Another procession takes the bride and groom to their new home, which the bride is supposed to enter without touching the threshold. In traditional child weddings, which still take place in some parts of rural India, the bride goes to her husband's home for three days, after which she returns to her family until she is old enough to live with her husband.

going through any formal marriage ceremony at all. In the West, this is looked on as a modern phenomenon: in the 19th and early 20th centuries such 'consensual marriage', when it did occur, was cause for comment, if not outright scandal. But such alliances have existed in a variety of cultures throughout history: they are not the preserve of modern civilization. It is true to say, however, that they usually represent a variant from the norm: there are few if any societies that do not have some form of established marriage ceremony.

There are many reasons why people decide to live together without marking the event with a ceremony. It may be that they feel that the available ceremony is not relevant to them – the religious or economic terms in which it is couched might not seem right. Or it might be that while the couple aspire to a ceremonial wedding, they cannot afford this and so decide to live together as man and wife until they can do so. Such a reason is often put forward in parts of the Caribbean in which lavish marriage festivities carry much prestige.

Even when a feeling of irrelevance makes people reject a formal marriage ceremony, many couples still feel the need for some sort of ritual acknowledgement of their relationship. Sometimes it can be something as simple as throwing a party for a group of friends. Such an action can fulfil many of the functions of a traditional ceremony.

THE ROLES OF MARRIAGE

Marriage has many purposes: it can provide the forum for an economic deal between two families; it can offer the setting for the bringing up of children; it can represent a political alliance between peoples. Often the interplay between the relationship of two people and their position in the whole community, is what drives the ceremony. When two people are

WEDDING DANCES

Symbolic of harmony and the coming together of partners, dancing forms a fitting accompaniment to courtships and weddings all over the world. It is often the culmination of the wedding celebration and, in many cultures, the couple will begin the dancing, to be gradually joined by all the other guests. Such dances are collective: everyone shares in the optimism and togetherness that are typical of a successful wedding.

DANCE OF THE WODAABE MEN

Dancing often plays an important part in courtship, and it can bring people together in a variety of ways. One of the more formalized examples of this is seen in the showy dance that the young men of the Wodaabe people of Niger perform to attract a partner. As they circle, each man hopes to catch the eye of a young woman.

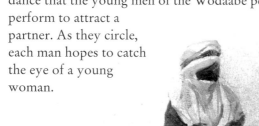

OLD AND YOUNG

Most big wedding celebrations unite the different generations in the joy of the dance.

allowed to make their own choice, they cannot ignore society (there is the feast to give, the procession to tread, the price to pay). When the marriage is instigated by parents or elders, the individual still has to be considered (the couple have individual obligations, and may have the final say in their acceptance of the partner). All these elements, and more, are reflected in the rich variety of rituals and customs surrounding marriage the world over.

DANCE OF THE CZECH MARRIED WOMEN
A Czech bride's female married relatives perform a special boisterous dance of honour for the bride. These women are dressed in their traditional national costumes, now only worn for special celebrations.

DANCE OF THE CAJUN BRIDESMAIDS
In New Orleans the sisters of the bride and groom perform a dance that is supposed to satirize their unmarried status. They stand on washtubs and wave brooms that have been decorated with ribbons, to the delight of all the company.

Death and funerals

Death is perhaps the most difficult and traumatic of human passages, not only for the person approaching death, but also for those who survive. The challenges it poses to human understanding are many. What happens to the deceased? What will life be like without those who are close to us? What will the experience be like for ourselves? Does life continue in any form after death? These are vital questions, but ones that are impossible to answer. While they cannot answer these questions, rituals can at least prepare us for the shock of death and ease us through the process of bereavement. Death is one of the universal human experiences and has inspired rituals and customs in every human culture.

These rituals go back to the very beginnings of human existence. Archaeologists working on the earliest human settlements often come across burial sites. Even the Neandertals, the early humans who lived in Europe and the Middle East between 100,000 and 40,000 years ago, buried their dead. What is striking about these burials is that they had obviously been carried out in a way that had little to do with the utilitarian needs of disposing of the body. Even in the most ancient cemeteries there is evidence of such customs as burying grave goods with the deceased, of arranging the body in a specific position, of mutilating or decorating the body in some way, or of leaving some ritual offering in the grave. For example, in a Neandertal burial of a child at Teshik Tash in Russia, the body was put in a shallow pit and pairs of goat horns were arranged in a circle around it; a fire was lit beside the grave.

The fact that such actions go back so far in human history should not be a surprise. Death has certainly inspired some of the high points of artistic expression. The poet W H Auden

LAST RITES
From the earliest times, when people were buried with their possessions, death has been marked with special funeral ceremonies that have provided a means of ensuring a good passage to the next life as well as a focus for mourning.

said that poets 'seem to be more generally successful at writing elegies than at any other literary genre'. Composers as diverse as Mozart, Verdi and Berlioz produced some of their greatest music in their settings of the Requiem Mass. Artists from the sculptors of medieval Burgundy to the Post-Impressionist painters have created out of death some of their most moving and disturbing images. Death is the ultimate human experience, and possibly the most challenging artistic subject. Perhaps the anticipation of death and the process of mourning are the experiences we share most closely with our earliest ancestors. In the ancient world as now, the ceremonies and customs surrounding death are one of the most fascinating aspects of human culture.

ANCIENT VIEWS OF THE AFTERLIFE

Many people in the secular western world today are used to thinking of death as the end, as a personal extinction. But religious people usually see death very differently, commonly as the beginning of a new phase of existence.

The latter view has history on its side, since the evidence is that this is how death was viewed almost everywhere until quite recently.

In many early human cultures tools and pots were left beside the dead, implying a belief that the dead live on in some way and that they need these objects in the afterlife. Some cultures decorated the bodies of the deceased with red ochre, this application of the colour of life to the corpse could have been to revivify it for the next phase of its existence.

Other cultures of the ancient world even made human sacrifices on the death of an important person: the royal deceased of Ur in Mesopotamia took their servants with them to the afterlife. Other traditions equipped the deceased for their journey to the next world in a variety of ways: ancient Greek corpses were buried with a coin to pay Charon, the ferryman who took them across the River Styx, and honey cakes for Cerberus, the terrifying dog at the gates of Hades. The coffins of ancient Egyptians sometimes bore a plan of the route to the underworld, while others contained a copy of the Book of the Dead, which contained spells that might be helpful to the deceased during their journey.

Notwithstanding such aids on the journey, admittance to the afterlife was not automatic in every culture. The deceased was often subjected to some sort of test before being allowed in. Sometimes this was a moral test based on the person's former life. The ancient

Egyptians, for example, believed that the dead person had to go through an elaborate ritual at the entrance to the next world. The heart, which contained a record of all the person's past deeds, would be weighed. Assessor gods would interrogate the dead person, accusing him or her of numerous crimes, which the person would deny. If the deceased told the truth, Thoth, the Ibis-headed god of wisdom, would declare that the person was 'true of voice' and he or she would pass through into

VIEWS OF THE AFTERLIFE

From ancient Egyptians to modern Christians, people have believed in some form of afterlife, and this belief has made last rites some of the most important of social rituals. For many people, the idea of the soul passing to the next world, whether through the flames of a funeral pyre or from a body exposed on a tall platform, is a powerful way of explaining what happens to us after we die. The Egyptians, like many early peoples, put grave goods in their tombs, so that the deceased had everything that was needed in the next world. Medieval Christians also saw the funeral service as an entry into the afterlife. Today, even for those who do not believe in life after death, such last rites remain, for the mourners, a vital part of coping with bereavement.

the kingdom of Osiris. For the untruthful, there was the awful fate of having one's heart devoured by a goddess called the 'Devourer of the Dead'. A number of later religions – for example, Zoroastrianism, Christianity and Islam – also encompass the idea of judgement of the dead.

Basic beliefs like these about the afterlife and its influence on the living world colour many of the diverse customs and rituals surrounding death that are still practised today. It is notable that the influence of the afterlife is often held to extend beyond the grave. Spirits are widely respected and even feared. An old West African custom is to pass a young baby over the coffin of an aged relative. This is believed to deter the dead person's spirit from interfering with the child.

PREPARING FOR DEATH

As is appropriate for the ultimate event in human life, rituals surrounding death often begin before death itself, as the person prepares

LOSING A LOVED ONE
Bereavement can be a devastating and lonely experience – although rituals can do something to allay the loneliness.

to die and the relatives prepare to face a new phase in their own existence. There are numerous superstitions that predict death after certain signs. A dog howling at the house of a sick person, the departure of crickets that have long lived near someone's house, or the appearance of mysterious flames (probably ignited marsh gas) are all examples of supposed portents of death.

Many cultures set great store by correct preparation for death. This may begin long before death. In some parts of India, for example, it is traditional for elderly people to give up their possessions and live their last years or months in poverty. When death seems to be close, Muslims are traditionally placed so that they face Mecca. Catholic Christians confess their sins and, on receiving absolution, are annointed with consecrated oil. The tradition in China was to help the dying person into a sitting position, which was held to make it easier for the soul to leave the body. The person's hair would be shaved, their body washed and nails cut. And the Murngin of Arnhem Land in northern Australia help the dying person into the land of the dead with songs invoking their ancestors. In their different ways, rituals like these ease the dying person from the secular to the spiritual realm, from the land of the living to the next world.

Such rituals help the dying person to face death, giving reassurance that in using the correct rite, their passage will be eased, that they will be accepted into the afterlife. They also help the survivors to face up to the loss of their loved one in the knowledge that the deceased will have a good passage.

There are other motives for a careful preparation – for example, the dying person and their relatives might be making the required social and financial arragements to ensure a stable future. Occasionally, it is simply a matter of sorting out the succession. In Micronesia, for example, the Ulithians gather around the dying man to hear him

TIWI FUNERAL, BATHURST ISLAND

The importance of artistic activity for Australian Aborigines is reflected in the rituals accompanying a funeral of one of the Tiwi people of Bathurst Island, off northern Australia.

CEREMONIAL POSTS

A skilled carver makes ceremonial posts out of bloodwood, a hard timber that is not vulnerable to rot or attack by termites. There may be as many as 12 such posts at one funeral. When the post is carved, it is blackened in a fire to prepare it for painting. An artist draws special designs on each post. He uses pigments such as ochre and pipeclay mixed with water. His brush is a stick, the end of which he has chewed to give a fibrous tip that holds the paint.

PROTECTIVE DISGUISES

Tiwi men singe their body hair in a pre-funeral purification ritual that protects them from injury and attack by spirits. Face-painting is an important preparation for the ritual. The Tiwi believe that if they do not disguise themselves, the spirit of the deceased will try to take loved ones away with him. Beards are sometimes stiffened with sticky sap and sometimes false beards are used.

DANCING

There are numerous dances at the funeral ceremony. One involves a ceremonial basket that is later left on the grave. There are also dances that depict the ancestor spirits of the participants. At the climax of the ceremony, some of those present may cut their heads with knives and break down in grief.

declare who will receive his goods when he dies. Sometimes such preparations are designed to bring the circumstances of the death itself out into the open. In the Transvaal, the BaVenda people come to the bedside of the dying to avoid being suspected of any sort of complicity in the death. Such customs clearly help to foster stability at a difficult time.

IMMEDIATELY AFTER DEATH

The period that follows straight after death carries its own specific customs and practices. Some of these are mysterious in their origins and purposes and seem to be mainly used as punctuation marks to signal the moment of death. Customs that were once widespread in various parts of Europe, such as removing a tile from the roof or emptying all the water vessels in the house, seem to belong to this

category. So too does the tradition, observed in some European countries of stopping all the clocks in the house at the time of death

In addition to such commemorative rites, there are many others designed to address the question of what one actually does with the corpse. Again, in most cultures, there is an emphasis on correctness, with often highly elaborate prefuneral preparation of the body. The complex mummification rituals of ancient Egypt are perhaps the most famous example. But other societies, such as that of ancient Peru, have used mummification, and still others have alternative means of preserving or decorating the corpse.

Washing, shaving, and grooming the corpse are common in many societies. Removing the internal organs, decorating the body with dyes such as turmeric or ochre, the use of perfumes, and adorning the corpse with clothing and

JAZZ FUNERAL, NEW ORLEANS

In many parts of the world, people adapt rituals to their local culture. One example of this is the jazz funeral of New Orleans. In this city of music, bands and combos of all sorts take to the streets to join the funeral procession or play from the sidewalks as the hearse passes by. On the way to the cemetery the music is solemn, but as the mourners return, the musicians perform what they know best – riotous, upbeat jazz that will perhaps help everyone back to an optimistic frame of mind.

jewellery are among the other mortuary customs. The closing of the eyes is a tradition that is observed in many cultures.

MARKS OF MOURNING

While all this is being done, whether by a priest or professional mortician, the deceased's family and friends give vent to their grief – in other words, they become mourners. There is often something unbridled about the ritual of mourning, a notable contrast to the formalized way in which the corpse is treated. In many cultures, the beating of breasts, tearing of hair, and loud and continuous wailing tell passers-by that there has been a death in the neighbourhood. On some occasions, professional mourners are also widely employed to add to the chorus of grief.

Such traditions are an acknowledgement of the overwhelming emotions that bereaved people usually experience. Frequently these feelings do not arise straight away. A time of shock and silence often follows a death, and it is common for people to carry on speaking of the deceased in the present tense, and to admit that they cannot believe that the death has taken place. As the realization comes, so do confusing emotions, from pain and bewilderment to guilt. The rituals of weeping and wailing are both a way of encouraging this grief to emerge from the experience of shock, and a way of expressing the confusing emotions themselves.

Mourning is rarely simply a matter of venting grief in tears. There are many other ways in which the bereaved can express their sorrow. One is by changing their outward appearance. In the West, it was traditional to wear black at the funeral and for some time afterwards. Nowadays, subdued clothing is thought to be adequate, although in many places, especially the Mediterranean countries, widows still keep to their black 'weeds', in some cases, for the rest of their lives. In other

BEFORE THEIR TIME
The death of a young person is sometimes marked in a special way. Although the grief of any bereaved person can be overwhelming, there is something particularly poignant about the death of a child.

SPECIAL CEREMONIES
There may be special ceremonies for babies who are stillborn. In Japan Buddhist parents may offer statues, sometimes dressed like children, and brightly coloured pinwheels. A priest prays before these offerings.

DEATH OF A BRIDE
This young Romanian woman, who died before she was married, is dressed as a bride for her funeral. Wedding vows are even recited at the funeral, in an attempt to take the deceased through the full cycle of her natural life.

DRESS FOR MOURNING

Special funeral garb is prescribed in most cultures. This is just a small sample of the many different types from around the world. Rules of dress may not always be observed to the letter.

EUROPE
The traditional costume of the southern European widow, is a black dress, often with a black veil or headcloth. Black has been linked with mourning in the West at least since the time of the Romans. Those attending western Christian funerals are expected to wear sombre garments.

INDONESIA
Muslim women in Indonesia don white veils for funerals.

JEWISH TRADITION
Jewish men let their hair grow and remain unshaven.

TAIWAN
A simple robe or dress of a hessian-like material, with a white headdress marks the Taiwanese mourner.

IRELAND
An Irish funeral procession follows the coffin.

CHINA
The Hei Miao people wear traditional black costumes.

BATHURST ISLAND
The Tiwi people disguise themselves with body paint at funerals.

SULAWESI
An elaborate headdress is worn at Toradja funerals.

cultures, white is the traditional colour for funeral wear and mourning.

Where clothes do not carry the message of mourning, special body paint can do so. Andaman islanders paint their bodies with yellow ochre and olive-green clay, using different patterns of stripes to show their relationship to the deceased. Bones were also traditionally worn in memory of the deceased. The Tiwi people of Bathurst Island off the northern Australian coast also use body paint. In this case it is considered to be a form of disguise. The dead are thought to return to take their friends and relatives away with them. Mourners are therefore in danger and need to cover up their identity.

There are many other traditional symbols of mourning. In some places the hair is allowed to grow long and untidy. Male Jewish mourners do not shave during the *shiva*, or traditional week of mourning, and will not cut their hair for a month after the death. In other cultures the hair is shaved. In some Melanesian islands, for example, it was the custom to wear an item called a *sogere*, a train of grass attached to the neck and extending down the mourner's back almost to the ground. At later stages in mourning, it would be replaced by a shorter version. Mourners might also smear their bodies with mud. In other cultures it is customary to cover the face with a veil.

Mourners in many societies live a more self-denying life than usual. They may go without certain foods and abstain from sex. A funeral feast might be a frugal affair, with only specific dishes permitted. However, in some societies the funeral is a lavish feast.

Food can also have a special significance attached to it in funerary rites. There was a custom in Bavaria, for example, in which cakes were left on the dead body before they were baked. Those who ate the cakes were held to have absorbed some of the virtues of the deceased. By contrast, in Wales, there was a custom called 'sin-eating', in which a mourner would eat food that had been passed over the body. The deceased's sins were supposed to enter the food and were thus consumed by the mourner.

The diverse customs of mourning in which the mourners are bound by traditional rules that lay down how one behaves, and usually the length of time for mourning. Whether the period is deemed to last for a few days after the death or for much longer, such regulation helps the bereaved come to terms with their grief and indicates the point at which they can resume a normal role in the community.

The vigil

The tradition of the vigil, in which mourners keep watch beside the corpse, can have several social uses. It can be a commemoration of the deceased, a chance to pay one's last respects, and, at the most basic level, a making public of the fact that the person is actually dead.

In many cultures it is thought necessary to

Small namba people
The presence of the spirit world is vividly portrayed in a funeral ritual of the Small Namba people of the island of Malekula in the New Hebrides.

Mask of death
The body of the deceased lies for a year on a funeral platform. After this time the skull is removed from the body and covered with a mixture of reddish clay and plant fibres, modelled to resemble the deceased. A body is made of wood, and the two are joined together. The patterns on the body indicate the social rank of the deceased.

Funeral dances
There are some ten days of dancing, after which the effigy is processed around the funeral area.

Evocation of spirits
A 'spirit' appears from the jungle. It is covered in fern leaves that have been blackened with smoke and its head is shrouded in spiders' webs.

Three more similar 'spirits' appear, together with two men painted red and whites. The painted men whip the mourners until they and the 'spirits' are given yams and depart.

Funeral meats
A pig is killed and pieces of meat are given to all present. The ceremony is finally at an end.

TORADJA PEOPLE, SULAWESI

At the funeral of a high-ranking Toradja man from Sulawesi in Indonsesia, as many as 16 buffaloes must be sacrificed. The funeral festival is held after the deceased has lain in state in his own house for several months.

OFFERINGS

Hundreds of people come to the funeral, many bringing buffaloes, others bringing pigs strung up on poles. As they arrive, the guests process around the central area of the village.

ENTERTAINMENT

People in brightly coloured headdresses perform songs and dances. These are in the form of prayers to ancestor spirits; they are also highly entertaining.

OFFICIAL DEATH

Meanwhile, the deceased rests, as he has done for months, inside his own house. Four men take the dead body and toss it in the air, chanting, before lowering it to the floor. Its feet point south, towards heaven. The man is now truly dead. He will remain here for months more.

RITUAL MOURNING

As ritual mourning begins, men and women take up separate songs and dances and buffaloes are sacrificed. On the second day there are buffalo fights.

BURIAL

Months later, the remains are carried in a red and gold funerary bag, togther with an effigy called a *tau-tau*, up a pole to a grave in the cliff side.

guard the corpse at all times. For some peoples, such as some of those living in Indonesia, the mourners are standing by to help the soul as it recovers form the shock of death. In other societies, the body is being guarded from the spirits. In still others it is being guarded from other living humans.

The vigil is also valuable because it helps to accustom the survivors to the facts and realities of death. There is nothing more frightening than the unknown, and death is in one sense unknowable. But getting close to the physical presence of death helps to reassure those left behind, and perhaps even moves them nearer

to coming to terms with their own death. Sitting by the corpse, visiting to pay one's respects, taking an active part in the preparation of the body for the funeral all serve this purpose. In some places in northern England, the custom of touching the dead has survived. Some have interpreted it as protecting the toucher from haunting, others see it as a mark of respect for the deceased. In the latter form it may be related to the old belief that a corpse will bleed if it is touched by its murderer.

Customs that were said to ease the departure of the soul were important in many

Christian countries where pagan traditions also lived on. Practices such as opening doors and windows, stopping clocks, and covering mirrors, were all said to make the departure of the soul easier. A related custom was to leave the door of the house open when the corpse and mourners left for the funeral. Tears in a dying person's room were said to delay the departure of the soul.

In many regions, from Ireland to the southern United States, from Burma to the islands of the South Seas, corpses lie in state, often in or near the home of the deceased or the bereaved. Even where it is not the norm for ordinary people, the bodies of celebrities and high-ranking politicians, for example, are often allowed to lie in state as a way of giving the community as a whole the opportunity to express its grief. In some places, the body lies in its coffin, in a quiet room, with religious symbols and mementoes around it. Elsewhere the body is set in a chair, specially made for the purpose. This is the tradition in some parts of New Guinea and in the Philippines. The Koita people of New Guinea, for example, would place the body outside in a chair, break up the person's possessions and place them around it. In the Philippines, death chairs are traditional among the Igorot people, while the Tinguian custom would be to prop the deceased up against one wall of the room.

BURIAL OF THE DEAD

From the earliest times, burial in the ground seems to have been one of the most widespread methods of disposing of the corpse and burials continue to be practised all over the world today. No one knows the orignal reasoning for such a choice but it is so long-standing as to seem perfectly natural. The ecological and symbolic reasons that may be expressed today for returning the dead to the earth that sustained us in life, are also given voice in ancient texts – 'You are dust, and to dust you

shall return', as the Old Testament (Genesis) of the Bible puts it. The imperatives both of basic hygiene and of giving the dead the best chance of rest are also fulfilled by burial.

In some cultures, burial is the only acceptable way of disposing of the body. Muslims, for example, believe in the resurrection of the body after death and therefore bury their dead. Before burial, the body is normally washed and wrapped in a shroud. Special prayers are said during the burial, which is usually attended only by men. Women have another role to play in the rites of death. They visit the grave regularly, sometimes for years after the person's death.

Burial is also a traditional ritual for Christians, although cremation is also widely practised. There is usually a brief service by the grave, often preceded by a church service.

The site of the burial is often important. In the Christian West people are familiar with the concept of consecrated ground. In other societies, such as in some traditional cultures in western Africa, people might be buried beneath the floors of their homes. The position or orientation of the corpse can also be important. Muslims, for example, are buried with their right side towards Mecca. Another key factor is the timing of the burial. Jewish law requires burial to take place as soon as possible, preferably within 24 hours of death. For Christians timing is less critical; funeral rites normally take place four or five days after death.

CREMATION

Burial is not the only method of disposing of the dead. Cremation is also an ancient ritual. It remains the favoured method among Hindus, Buddhists, certain native North American peoples, and nomadic peoples who do not want to leave their dead behind. It has the particular advantage in some areas of preventing animals from attacking or eating the

NORTHERN BUDDHIST FUNERAL, SIKKIM

In this Himalayan region, Buddhists use a funeral ritual that is designed to ease the deceased through a series of stages between death and rebirth, and to ensure a favourable new life.

THE PROCESSION

A long procession winds towards the funeral pyre. Near the front, someone carries a parasol, indicating that the deceased is a member of the royal family. Close behind is the body on its bier. A priest or lama holds a white scarf that is attached to the body.

ARRIVAL AT THE PYRE

As the procession arrives at the pyre, it is welcomed by blasts on trumpets. The pyre itself is a stone or mud-brick structure with an open top and a hollow interior in which the fire is made. The bier is placed on the pyre. Wreaths of flowers are added around the base.

LIGHTING THE PYRE

The pyre is lit and offerings of consecrated oil and clarified butter are poured on, using pans attached to the ends of long poles. The red-robed monks chant as the remains of the deceased and the bier fall down into the fire.

corpse. In some cultures it is also seen as helping the soul to escape from the body so that it can travel into the afterlife.

Cremation is an essential ritual of Hinduism. Hindus believe in reincarnation and that the soul passes through various, not necessarily human, bodies. The body that the soul occupies is influenced by conduct in the previous life. At the time of death the soul is considered to be trapped inside the skull. It must therefore be released with the aid of a sacred fire in the ceremony of cremation.

Before a Hindu funeral pyre is lit, a male relative of the deceased walks three, five or seven times around the pyre holding a piece of burning wood. He then lights the pyre and the son or sons of the deceased pray for the peace and rest of departed ancestors. (This, incidentally, is one reason why Hindus set so much store by the male line: only a son may perform this ritual). The fire, which is made fragrant with spices such as sandalwood, camphor or saffron, is made so that the maximum heat is directed at the skull. When this breaks, the soul is released and the relatives may leave the funeral. Professional mourners often remain. On the third day after the funeral,

PLATFORM GRAVE
In the northwestern United States widows mourn a chief. His body has been placed on a canoe with the head pointing towards the sea.

VICTIM OF WAR
Even among the violence and chaos of the battlefield, the dead are given their last rites with as much dignity as possible. Here a group of soldiers mourns a comrade killed in Vietnam. The grave is marked with a makeshift cross.

the ashes are gathered up and taken to be scattered in a river.

Buddhists also often cremate their dead. The Buddha himself was cremated and his followers, particularly the southern Buddhists (or Theravadins) of Burma, Sri Lanka and Thailand, use the same ritual. In Burma, for example, monks come to comfort mourners and chant sacred texts to them. The chanting, which continues as the body is prepared for the pyre, helps the good energies of the deceased to be released. The monks also come to the funeral itself. Here, relatives and friends make donations – often of food and candles – to the monks. The resulting goodwill is considered to help the spirit of the deceased.

A notable use of fire after death occurs among Romany peoples. Romanies do not in

general like to inherit from the dead, and a gypsy who is near to death will give away many possessions. When death finally comes there is usually a religious funeral. The deceased's remaining possessions, including the caravan, are burnt.

In a ceremony performed by the Kuku-kuku people of New Guinea, fire is used in a ritual of mummification in which the corpse is smoked over a fire. After a period of mourning lasting several days, the fire begins to dry out the body. Finally, when the body is fully desiccated, it is displayed in a place of honour.

PLATFORM GRAVES

Another alternative to burial or cremation is to expose the corpse to the elements and to predators. This has never been a widespread practice. Some Australian Aborigines place corpses in trees or on platforms; some native North Americans used platforms, as did the ancient Persians, whose dead had their flesh quickly removed by vultures. The Persians' reason for exposing their dead in this way was to prevent the sacred elements (fire, earth and water) from being defiled by the corpse.

OTHER FUNERAL RITUALS

The transportation of the corpse from home to the place of burial or cremation inspires some of the most solemn rituals of all. In Hindu funerals there is frequently a procession headed by a man carrying a flaming torch started at the hearth of the deceased.

While the ancient practice of burying grave goods is rarely followed today – with the exception perhaps of the informal placing of a special memento in the grave by a mourner – many of the funeral rites described show that survivors still want to provide for the deceased.

Whatever is thought to have happened to the deceased's soul, many funeral customs underline the endurance of life on Earth, in spite of the death. This can be seen in many of the joyous dances that occur at the end of funerals. The western tradition of the wake, in the sense of a party rather than a bierside vigil, which can begin as a mournful gathering and end as a riotous party, is another example.

In secular cultures, particularly in the West, there is less emphasis on the religious aspect of the funeral ceremony. But there is still the need for some sort of ritual, some marking of the passing of a person from the world, some focus for the grief of those who are left behind, some meeting place for the people to share their memories of the deceased.

FRANCE
Slender cemetery lantern towers are seen in the Haute-Vienne region of France. The pyramidal cap originally contained a lamp that was always kept alight to mark the consecrated ground where the dead were buried.

TURKEY
The tapering gravestones of Muslim cemeteries mark the graves, which face towards Mecca. The stones are decorated with inscriptions and leaf and fruit motifs carved in relief.

TIBET
High on the Himalayas, stone cairn tombs are often adorned with flags inscribed with Buddhist prayers.

MARKING THE GRAVE

Whoever we are, whatever our culture, we expect our last resting place to be marked in some way – it is a way of keeping the memory of the deceased alive, and of providing a focus for those who wish to honour or remember the dead. Burial may take place in a cemetery, in a grave marked by a stone or by flags or a wooden canopy. Each form of grave marking adds to the dignity accorded the dead.

CHINA

Tall towers marked graveyards in China when ancestor worship flourished there in the early 20th century.

EUROPE

Crosses are the traditional marker for Christian graves. There are numerous forms, traditional in different areas, such as the Celtic cross, seen here. Christian symbols such as the fish may also appear.

BORNEO

Brightly decorated wooden canopies formed the traditional adornment of the graves of the Dusun people of coastal Borneo.

CENTRAL ASIA

Muslim nomads live in the Pamir mountains of Eastern Turkestan. They build mosque-like tombs for their dead.

SURVIVING

FROM HUNTING TO HEALING: SUPPLYING THE BASIC NEEDS OF LIFE

Survival: the very word conjures up our most fundamental needs, and perhaps the most fundamental of them all are good health and regular food. It is not surprising that these basic requirements have given rise to some of our most vital rituals and customs. People living traditional lifestyles are perhaps more acutely aware than those in the industrialized West of the precarious nature of a regular food supply, but food and health are important everywhere, and rituals of survival flourish in all societies. Some of the first ceremonies and customs to do with hunting, farming and eating were no doubt designed to placate the gods, who were thought to control the apparent caprice of the weather and the ever-changing seasons. Make an offering to the sun god before planting; offer some of the harvest to the gods; give thanks to the deity for food before eating. Rituals like these would seem to appease the gods, and make them smile on next year's harvest or next week's kill. Such customs still survive. Even in the West, we continue to celebrate the harvest and say grace on formal occasions.

Working together

There are also intensely practical reasons for the ceremonies that surround our survival. Collaboration is one of the greatest strengths of the human race. Whether we are out hunting for our food or bringing in the harvest, we can usually achieve a more abundant and more reliable food supply if we collaborate with our relatives and neighbours. Customs and rituals help to foster such co-operation. Rituals can also facilitate the process of sharing out the food, providing a framework for distribution that everyone accepts. This is particularly important where food is in short or irregular supply, whether hunted, gathered or farmed.

Healing powers

The healing arts have given rise to some of our most fascinating rituals and customs. Dances in which a shaman, that combination of priest and healer common in traditional societies, removes an evil spirit from a patient may seem to have little to do with physical illness, but apparently effect dramatic cures. Even western doctors are prepared to admit that such practices may help, perhaps by raising the patient's morale and belief in the cure.

Rituals, then, from the niceties of table manners to the life-and-death activities of healers, are at the very heart of our survival. They find us at our closest to the powers that foster life on Earth, from the sunshine that makes the crops ripen to the curative powers of a plant or human touch. They can be said, perhaps, to formalize our relationship with the forces of nature.

Hunting and harvesting

'Cherish us no grudge because we
have killed you. You have sense; you
see that our children are hungry'
*Native North American hunter to
his quarry*

Much human activity is concerned with the search
for food. In the earliest human societies and in
some traditional societies today, it was a question
of hunting animals and gathering plants. Even with
the coming of agriculture, by which people found a
more predictable way of supplying their needs,
producing food was no less labour-intensive and
no less vital. A failure of the food supply, whether
caused by bad weather, crop disease or simple bad
luck in the hunt, would mean certain hunger and
possible starvation.

The forces that affect the food supply, thereby
holding sway over human life and death, seem vast
in their power and often arbitrary in their actions.
It is not surprising, therefore, that people have
created rituals, indeed entire religions, around
procedures to ensure success in the hunt and
harvest. Such rituals are most common in
traditional societies, but there are also some
notable examples in the developed world. After all,
even modern methods of 'agribusiness' are reliant
on the same environmental forces as those that
dominate traditional lifestyles around the world.

PREPARING FOR THE HUNT

In societies that get their food by hunting and
gathering, it is usually the women who gather and
the men who hunt. In many parts of the world it is
possible to find edible plant material for much of
the year. During this time, the food gathered by the
women makes up the main food source,
supplemented when possible by meat from animals
that the men have killed. On the whole, gathering
is a reliable source of food – when one area is
exhausted, the people move on. The routine of
gathering is regular and, barring disasters, there
is enough to go around. There is, therefore,
little need for the assistance of special rituals to
guarantee the food supply.

But in the sparse winter season, there may be little available to the gatherer, and this is the time of the year in which the people are most likely to depend on hunting for survival. Hunting is usually a less reliable source of food than gathering, and hunters are more likely to use special rituals to help them than gatherers. Such rituals go back far into the past. The earliest known cave paintings are widely thought to be part of primitive hunting rituals in which the favoured quarry was drawn before a hunting expedition in the belief that this would make the real animals appear. Some authorities have even speculated that the paintings were part of some sort of pre-enactment ritual, in which missiles were thrown at the images of the animals. This may explain the marks and depressions around some of the pictures. Thus, by a sort of sympathetic magic, success in this ritual 'hunt' would lead to success in the real hunt.

Correct preparation for hunting is still held to be vital in many traditional societies. Every hunter makes ready his weapons before setting off. Of course, the correct weapons are essential and this is widely recognized. A boy of the African Hadza people, for example, is permitted to join the hunt provided that he can make or obtain properly made arrows. But having the correct weapons often means more than simply ensuring one has enough arrows or that one's knife is sharp. The East African Maasai warrior paints his shield with the correct patterns. The Inuit hunter often decorates his weapons with designs appropriate to the day's quarry. Some hunters in West Africa hang up quivers full of arrows in the trees before the hunt. Later, when the

TOOLS FOR THE JOB
The rituals of the hunt often include a show of respect for the prospective victim. This is not surprising, since no one is more aware than the hunter of the animal's skill in avoiding human pursuit and death. Such respect is sometimes reflected in the care with which hunters fashion their weapons. These Inuit harpoon heads, for example, are superbly crafted from bone. The hunters believe that the soul of the animal appreciates being hunted with a weapon of beauty. The soul of the dead animal is considered to be passed on to an unborn creature, so the knowledge of how it has been treated is passed on. The small harpoon head (above) is for seal hunting. The large harpoon head is for a still more formidable quarry, the walrus.

DIVIDING THE KILL
After the hunt comes the carve-up. The spoils may be divided according to need or priority may be given to the hunter who showed most bravery or to the one who actually made the kill. Here, !Kung hunters carve up an antelope.

arrows are taken down and used, their time up in the trees is held to help them on their upward journey towards their targets.

Dancing may be a part of the pre-hunt ritual, as used to be the case with the Vedda people of Sri Lanka. The hunters would dance around an arrow stuck in the ground, beating time on their flanks and invoking the spirit of Kande, a famous hunter. Many cultures make use of such pre-hunt dances.

There may also be rituals to find the best place to hunt. The Mistassini Cree people of North America, for example, have a 'shaking tent ritual' that shamans (priests or medicine men) use to find the location of game. A shaman enters a specially constructed tent and sings about the hunt. As he does so, the poles of the tent shake and the shaman thereby learns the best place for the hunters to go. Among many native North American peoples there are also drumming ceremonies that help the hunters to decide on the best location.

Drumming is believed to help the people to make contact with spirits who will guide the hunters to their quarry.

THE DIVISION OF THE SPOILS
At the end of the hunt, there are rituals to determine the appropriate division of the spoils. Hunting is often a cooperative venture, in which a group of men work together to trap their quarry. But, even in a joint enterprise, special honour might be due to one or two individuals, who have exhibited particular bravery, or whose aim was especially successful.

The Guayaki, who inhabit the tropical forests of Paraguay, have a custom that a hunter may not eat meat that he has caught himself. The Guayaki explanation for this is that a hunter who eats meat he has taken will become unlucky in hunting, but the custom also ensures that the whole group gets fed, not just the hunter and his close relatives. There are, however, also customs that protect the close family in certain circumstances. If the hunter brings in only a small amount of game, his wife and children are given priority.

Such customs of sharing exist among many hunting peoples. Many Inuit, for example, have precise rules about how to divide up a seal and to whom the different portions may be given. Such customs may extend to the division of fish and caribou meat in the relevant season. In some tribes, communal eating reinforces such customs.

When the hunt is unsuccessful, there are also rituals to perform. Many people believe that bad luck in the hunt is the result of the gods' displeasure, perhaps because the pre-hunt ceremonies were not performed properly.

So additional sacrifices may be required, or there may be a special post-hunt dance.

HUNTING RELIGIONS

The importance of hunting and the close relationship between people and the animals they hunt is revealed by many hunting religions. The ancient Greeks had a cult of the goddess Artemis, the virgin huntress who was patron of huntsmen under the name Agrotera; the Roman equivalent was the goddess Diana. Many modern peoples also have hunting deities. The Copper Inuit, for example, have a chief deity called Arnakapfaaluk, the 'big, bad woman', who lives in a cave at the bottom of the sea. She controls the sea animals and also influences Hila inua, the spirit of the air.

HUNTING FOR FUN
Even in places where there is no need to hunt for food, ancient methods of hunting are preserved as recreation. Deer hunters, like these from Scotland, people who shoot game birds and those who fish are all looking back to times when these activities were necessary for survival.

Elsewhere many religions and cults have an important hunting element. Among the Lele of the Kasai River in Africa, cult groups fulfil the dual function of promoting both fertility and good hunting. One of the most important cults is that of the pangolin. Scaled like a fish, climbing in the trees and reproducing in the human manner with one baby at a time, the pangolin seems to inhabit several worlds at once. It is also special because it seems to offer itself up to the hunter. When a hunter sees a pangolin in the forest, he taps it sharply on the back, making it roll itself up into an armoured ball. The hunter then waits quietly until the creature unrolls itself again, at which time he quickly kills it. The eating of this strange animal is held to bring success to the hunter and fertility to women.

Humans often seek to appropriate the strength of wild animals, and this is reflected in the practices of many hunting cults. In the islands of Melanesia, for example, the men hunt with dogs. They mix particles of ground-up crocodile tooth with the dog's food, or touch the dog's nose with the claw of a hawk, to transfer some of the qualities of these creatures to the dog.

Rituals of agriculture

Like their counterparts in hunting cultures, traditional agricultural rituals spring from cultures that are very close to the natural

MAASAI LION HUNT
Like many other hunting peoples, the Maasai have special rituals governing the decoration of shields, the use of headdresses, and the trophies that are handed out at the end of a hunt.

SYMBOLS OF BRAVERY
Each warrior carries a buffalo-hide shield that has been decorated to denote the section of the tribe to which he belongs. Circular patterns indicate acts of particular bravery - their use requires special permission.

LION-DANCE
Dances before a lion hunt include the Namba, in which dancers jump up in the air, landing stiff-legged. As they come down, they make sounds that are supposed to sound like a lion coughing.

GETTING READY
The hunters gather together. Many wear ostrich-feather headdresses. Those who have held the tail of a lion in a previous hunt may wear a lion's-mane headdress. The hunters move off in groups to look for lions in the scrub.

THE SUCCESSFUL HUNTERS
After the kill, the warriors gather around the defeated beast. The bravest hunters are given the lion's tail, mane and paws.

JAPANESE RICE-TRANSPLANTING CEREMONY

A traditional ceremony for the transplanting of rice is held every year on the first Sunday in June in some parts of rural Japan. It honours a crop that has been the staple food in Japan for more than two thousand years. The ceremony largely died out after the abolition of the feudal system in Japan in 1900, but was revived in 1930. Its continuance is now encouraged by the Japanese Government.

FLOWER COSTUMES
Dressed in enormous hats decorated with arches of flowers, dancers process through the streets.

DANCES FOR THE SPIRITS
Children act out dances that portray legendary events. These were originally intended to amuse and entertain the spirits of the Shinto religion.

A GREAT PROCESSION
In the middle of the day there is a procession that includes oxen carrying silver and gold-coloured saddles and banners that show their owners' family emblems.

SMOKE-BORNE PRAYERS
Women pray before a fire of rice straw, summoning the rice-god Sanbai-sama. The smoke is supposed to carry their prayers towards heaven.

PLANTING
Working in a perfectly co-ordinated line, guided by a cord stretched across the field, the women bend down to plant the rice seedlings. In the background, musicians accompany their labour on pipes and drums.

world. There is a widespread belief that humans and the gods must work in close cooperation to attain both success in the fields and a more general harmony. The idea of sacrifice to the gods is related to this notion. Nowhere was this clearer than in the religion of the Aztecs, who sacrificed humans to the Sun god in return for good harvests, fragrant flowers, tobacco, and good health.

Many peoples have specific ways of asking the gods to help them with their agriculture. Among native North American peoples, for example, rainmaking ceremonies. are common The Navaho believe that drought can be the result of evil or improper thoughts. Such a drought can be remedied with a rainmaking ceremony, but this will only work if the rites are performed correctly and without the bad thoughts that caused the initial problem.

The planting of crops is also sometimes attended by special rituals, designed to ensure a successful yield. Traditional Japanese planting ceremonies invoking the rice god were celebrated regularly and have been revived in some places – an indication that such customs have a certain potency, even in a society as technologically advanced as Japan.

Other milestones of the agricultural calendar were also attended with festivities. May Day, for example, was widely celebrated in Europe as the time when flocks and herds were turned on to their summer grazing land. Dancing around maypoles, the crowning of a young woman as May Queen, making garlands of may (hawthorn) – all celebrations of both agricultural and human fertility – were also common in England.

Harvest home

The customs of harvest would start as soon as the crops began to be gathered in. In many societies, the first fruits of the harvest were especially significant. The ancient Jews were told to take the first fruits to the temple as an offering to God. In England, a loaf made from the first corn to be harvested would be taken to church to be used in the Mass. The Anglo-Saxons called this service Hlaf-masse, from which the English word Lammas was derived. So Lammas-tide, celebrated at the beginning of August, became one of the important traditional festivals in the English calendar, especially in the countryside.

Rituals that relate specifically to the harvest often take place in the fields themselves, as the crop is being cut. This was the case with some of the traditional English harvest customs. Often special care would be devoted to the cutting of the last few ears of corn, the binding together of the last sheaf, or the carting away of the last load of corn. The young woman who cut the last sheaf might be dubbed 'harvest queen'. Frequently the removal of the last load would entail a procession as the

A CENTRAL EUROPEAN HARVEST
As the last of the corn is cut and loaded onto the cart, the whole village gathers for a procession to celebrate getting the harvest home.

workers returned with it from the fields. The harvest queen would often be decked with flowers and helped up onto the cart to ride with the corn. Elsewhere, triumphant songs would be sung by the workers, and in at least one place buckets of water were thrown over the harvesters as they went through the village.

Customs like this fulfilled several functions. They showed the community's relief or triumph that a good harvest had been got in –

everyone would be well fed for another season. The celebrations allowed people to 'let their hair down' and have a good time after a sustained period of hard, backbreaking work. The symbolism associated with fertility such as the thrown water, expressed, perhaps, the hope that the fields would be fruitful next year too. The making of the intricate, decorative constructions known as corn dollies was also a rite to encourage the fertility of the soil. Corn

CORN DOLLIES

The belief that plants have as much of a spirit as humans and animals is common in traditional societies. The English tradition of making effigies called corn dollies with the last of the corn reflects the belief that the spirit of the corn inhabited the last of the crop to be cut. It was held that a 'doll' made from the last of the corn would keep the corn spirit alive through the winter until the next crop was sown, thereby ensuring another good harvest.

The corn dolly (which might be given an affectionate name like 'The Old Wife' or 'Granny') would traditionally be made in the fields as soon as the last corn had been cut. In a typical mixture of Christian and pre-Christian rituals, the corn dolly was often taken into church for the harvest service. Later it would be hung in the barn. Corn dollies are still made, although those who create these intricate constructions do so more to revive a rural craft than to preserve the corn spirit.

dollies, harvest queens, and effigies made from the last sheaf all hark back to representations of the corn goddess Ceres and alert us again to the sense of closeness between the human, natural and supernatural worlds common in traditional agricultural communities.

Another widespread traditional celebration is the harvest feast – an occasion for enjoyment and release after hard work, combined with a time for thanksgiving to the gods for a successful crop. The ancient Inca harvest celebration showed this blend of religion and merrymaking very well. After a period of fasting, large numbers of llamas and other animals and birds would be slaughtered, the statues of the gods would be anointed with the blood of the animals, and a great feast would take place.

Even where the local religion requires no

sacrificial offerings like this, there is still likely to be a thanksgiving meal. European harvest feasts have been replaced in many places by the more sober Christian harvest festival. Baskets of produce are brought in to decorate the church and a special service is held to give thanks to God for the successful harvest.

The Jews have a number of festivals with origins in the rituals of harvesting. Shavuoth, the Festival of Weeks occurs at the end of the barley harvest and the beginning of the wheat harvest. Foods such as blintzes (pancakes stuffed with cheese) are eaten and the synagogues are decorated with flowers. Shavuoth also marks the time when Moses received the Ten Commandments, so thanks is given for the Torah as well as for the fruits of the harvest.

Sukkot, the Jewish Festival of Booths or Tabernacles, takes place at the time of the grape harvest. The feast is one at which people give thanks to God for the food that grows in garden and field. Palm branches, flowering myrtle and etrog (a citrus fruit) are traditionally offered in the synagogue. Prayers for rain end the festival.

These Jewish festivals are celebrated on the same days all over the world, for their significance goes further than the timing of the harvest in Israel. Similarly, Chinese people in many places celebrate Chung Ch'iu, the festival of the Moon Goddess, on the 15th day of the 8th month of the Chinese calendar. Thanks for the harvest, celebration of the Moon deity, and the eating of moon cakes are all important elements in the celebration.

The rituals of both hunting and farming then, are powerful forces for social unity. They bring communities together in recognition of the universal importance of the need to ensure success in the search for food.

SUKKOT
The Jewish feast of the Tabernacles, or Sukkot, recalls the journeyings of the people of Israel through the wilderness. In addition to remembering the journeys of the Israelites, Sukkot is also a harvest festival, during which prayers of thanksgiving for the harvest are offered. The people build temporary wooden booths covered with branches. Big enough to accommodate a table, the interiors of the booths are decorated with fruit. The family takes its meals inside the booth for seven or eight days.

Eating and drinking

There are perhaps more customs to do with eating than any other human activity. In addition to the mainly everyday customs described in this chapter, food has an important part to play in many of the rituals discussed elsewhere in this book – including rites of passage, religious ceremonies, rituals of gift-giving, and so on. But even the least formal family meal is ritualized. The arrangement of the table, the order of the courses, the way the food is served, the way we show our appreciation of the meal – all these things are likely to have a ritual element.

Such rituals are indications of the key role of food in our lives: it is the stuff of our survival. Therefore it is not surprising that it is traditional in many cultures to give formal thanks for food – either to the host or the cook, or directly to God, by saying grace. Furthermore, there is something magical about cooking – the way food changes its appearance and taste when it is prepared and cooked must have seemed like alchemy to our ancestors. Food can have important symbolic and cultural meanings, too. Sharing food can cement friendship and may even indicate a sharing of religious beliefs.

RELIGIOUS RULINGS

Perhaps the most familiar food customs are those linked to particular religions. From the ancient Egyptians to modern Hindus, food has long been used in offerings to the gods. Many of the best known religious food customs involve specific rules about what can be eaten, and even how food should be prepared. Among orthodox and traditional believers, these rules are generally looked upon as laws, although other groups may adhere less strictly to them. The culinary rules of Judaism are some of the most specific. For example: only those animals with cloven hooves and which also chew the cud may be eaten (cattle, sheep, goats and deer); only the forequarters of the animal may be eaten; only fish with scales and fins are allowed. Furthermore, meat and dairy foods must not be consumed at the same meal and should be prepared separately using separate utensils. There are also rules about

FEAST AS CELEBRATION
From wine at the grape harvest to traditional puddings and sweetmeats at major festivals, food and drink have always played a vital part in celebrations.

the way animals may be slaughtered. Foods, in short, are divided into the *kosher* (fit to eat) and the *trayf* (unclean, not to be eaten). Observance of the sabbath prohibition of all work means that food must be prepared in advance of that day.

Muslim dietary regulations are laid down in the section of the Qur'an known as 'The Cow'. The faithful must eat neither pork nor blood and must not drink alcohol; there are special slaughter procedures that are in many respects similar to those of the Jewish faith.

Hindus are traditionally instructed that it is best not to kill or eat any animal; beef is forbidden completely; the cow is considered a sacred animal. The laws of Hinduism acknowledge that meat-eating is a widespread

SACRED COW
This animal is sacred to Hindus, who do not
eat its flesh.

human activity, but that it is better to abstain. Devout Hindus and Brahmins (those from the priestly caste) are therefore expected to be vegetarians. The caste system lays down who may eat with whom. A Brahmin, for example, may not eat with or take food from an untouchable.

Christians of the Roman Catholic faith are traditionally prohibited from eating meat on Fridays, serving fish instead on that day.

Christian sects, such as the Mormons and Seventh Day Adventists observe the sabbath strictly and prepare their sabbath food on the day before. These two sects also avoid drinking tea and coffee, and along with the Methodists abstain from alcohol.

Certain religious food customs reveal the rich symbolism that food can provide in many cultures. At the Jewish New Year, for example, bread and slices of apple are dipped in honey, indicating a wish for a sweet year. At Yom Kippur, the Day of Atonement, there is a fast. On the day before, *kreplach* (pancakes filled with meat) are eaten: they are said to symbolize stern judgement wrapped in mercy. In Eastern Orthodox countries, rituals involving food symbolism are widespread during Lent and Easter. Hardboiled eggs that are dyed red to represent Christ's blood are prepared during Lent and broken on the morning of Easter Sunday, recalling the opening of Christ's tomb. Elsewhere in Christian countries, sweet Easter eggs are relished by children.

Many Christian festivals have special foods. In southern Greece there are spiced Christmas breads, decorated with a hooked cross, and with walnuts embedded in the dough. The nuts are said to represent the virgin Mary; sometimes egg is used to make the cross. The use of eggs, which can be seen to symbolize fertility, in many Easter customs may hark back to earlier pagan celebrations of spring.

There are many reasons for these different religious dietary laws and customs. Symbolism is an obvious one. There are also good environmental reasons. The avoidance of pork, for example, is widespread in the Middle East among Muslims, Jews, and some Christians alike It may be that the origins of the taboo are as much to do with food hygiene as religion. Economic factors, have a strong influence in some cultures where little meat is eaten – for example, in China and Japan. Such considerations may also have been behind the

HONEY COLLECTORS, NEPAL

A food that is scarce and difficult to obtain, or that has special properties not found in other foods, is often highly valued. One such substance is honey. For thousands of years people have taken great risks to collect it. In some places in Nepal, men still make a perilous climb on rope ladders to reach this sweet and valuable food lodged in otherwise inaccessible cliffs.

A PERILOUS CLIMB

Starting at the top of the cliff, the man works his way slowly down the swinging rope ladder towards the bees' nest. Friends perch on a ledge above him to keep the ladder steady. Other colleagues light a fire at the base of the cliff to make smoke to calm the bees.

PREPARATION

Only certain men from the village who have learned the skills from their fathers are permitted to collect honey. Before setting out, the collector may sprinkle rice grains in the air while reciting the many names of the god of the forest. He may also sacrifice a chicken and search the entrails for omens. Such practices help guard against stinging.

THE HARVEST

A pole is stuck into the outer part of the nest, known as the brood comb, which is rich in wax. As this is prized away, the collector levers the honeycomb into a basket on the end of another pole. Meanwhile, bystanders at the base of the cliff hold pots and pans to collect the honey that spills. Later the honey will be shared out, according to the part each played in the collecting expedition.

demise of the pig in the Middle East. With the coming of farming, many forested areas were cleared and the pig began to lose its natural habitat and became rare. Finally, food customs can take hold because of one group's need to distinguish itself from others.

GIVING AND SHARING

Food customs that set a group apart also have the parallel effect of binding that group more closely together. Such an effect can be seen in many Buddhist communities, where lay people

are traditionally responsible for providing food for the monks. This is the consequence of many secular food customs, too. Sharing food is one of the most important ways in which people can express their friendship and solidarity and this is as true whether the meal is formal or informal. The recent revival of annual feasting in some southwestern French villages is a good example of social binding through food. So is a custom of the Wamiran

TEA CEREMONY, JAPAN

Sometimes the ceremonial aspect of eating and drinking becomes the most important part of all. Among Japanese Zen Buddhists, for example, tea drinking has a special significance. The careful ordering and measuring involved in the ritual of tea-making and tea-drinking have become part of a sort of meditation, a way to leave the everyday cares of the world behind and attain an inner harmony.

THE CEREMONY

The following is only a brief summary of what is a highly complex ceremony. Guests change into special clothes. They view the implements to be used and then crawl through a low door (to impose humility on all) before taking their seats. The host prepares the charcoal and lights the fire, which the guests examine. Then the host serves food, but does not eat. After an interlude, the *koicha* (thick tea) is prepared, poured into small bowls, and drunk. This is performed with care and grace. A further interlude is followed by the preparation and drinking of *usucha,* a less concentrated form of the same tea.

people of Papua New Guinea, who say that food must be shared with all who have set eyes on it – the exclusion of any such person is a mark of social rejection.

Food is also a powerful agent of reconciliation. 'Killing the fatted calf' is a well known Biblical saying. It is practised almost literally by the Gogo of Tanzania, who slaughter a goat to reconcile two people after a quarrel. The two parties must each eat half of the animal's liver.

Young people in the West today sometimes use food as an important way of expressing their membership of a peer-group. Whether it is a question of eating hamburgers and 'junk food' or expressing a preference for a 'high-energy' drink advertised by an Olympic athlete, the sense of belonging is confirmed.

Gifts of food can also be used to cement a relationship. There is an old rural Swedish custom in which people go around the village on Shrove Tuesday giving sweets, biscuits and buns to the children. People in the West give each other chocolate or some other luxury food to say 'you are special' or 'I love you'. Gifts of food are also common at occasions of feasting like Christmas. The gifts that businesses make to valued clients (cases of wine, bottles of whisky, local delicacies) are designed to work in the same way – in this case, cementing a commercial, rather than a personal relationship. It is also traditional in many societies to reciprocate the gift of hospitality by bringing a gift to one's host. Wine to drink with the meal is accepted with pleasure in many places – but not always in Spain, Portugal or Italy, where the host would be offended by the implication that such an essential has to be provided by the guest.

There may be an element of embarrassment in receiving a gift of food and the possible criticism of the host's hospitality that this may imply, and this is played on in some societies. The Massim people of New Guinea, for example, make lavish gifts of food to

BUTTER FESTIVAL, TIBET

For the Buddhist monasteries of Tibet, one of the greatest festivals of the year was the butter festival, held on the 15th day of the first moon. The highlight of the festival was the display of sculptures of Tibetan deities – brightly coloured constructions made completely of butter.

A BUTTER MOUNTAIN

Wealthy patrons of the monastery would donate thousands of kilograms of yak butter. This was mixed with powdered pigments of as many as 20 different colours.

COLD WORK

The monks would work hard for almost a month to mould the figures. The work had to be done in a cool room, and they had to dip their fingers repeatedly in cold water to mould the butter into the required shapes which was hard, uncomfortable work.

wrongdoers. Since the normal expectation is that one gift will be returned with another, the wrongdoer is given more than he can possibly return. The result is that his misdeed is highlighted and the injured party, by taking part in the gift-giving, has his or her honour restored. Gift-giving is discussed at greater length on pages 162–171.

FEASTING AND FASTING

Food plays a part in nearly all the types of celebrations described in this book. People acknowledge the celebratory nature of feasts by dressing up – the ancient Greeks wore wreaths to banquets; and in the West it is customary to dress up to go out to a restaurant. Feasts of the seasons, religious and secular festivals, and personal rituals such as birthdays and rites of passage – all are accompanied by special, often elaborate, meals.

Many are associated with specific dishes or types of food. Some of the most notable are national festivals. In Scotland, for example, and among Scots the world over, it is traditional to celebrate Burns Night on January 25, the anniversary of the birth of the poet Robert Burns. Haggis, the Scottish dish made from the offal of sheep or calf, oatmeal, suet and seasoning stuffed into a skin made from the animal's stomach, is the centrepiece of the meal. Much whisky, another Scottish speciality, is also consumed. In Germany, where the national drink is beer, the Oktoberfest is held annually in Bavaria

There are also traditional foods for personal celebrations. In Korea, children are given rice cakes and fruit on their birthdays. In Japan, lobster is a traditional birthday food: its bent back symbolizes old age and the hope for 'many happy returns'. Cakes are common at weddings and sugar or honey are often used to symbolize good fortune. This is said to be the origin of the sweet pastries and sugared almonds handed out at Lebanese weddings and at some Jewish ceremonies. Such symbolism is common everywhere. It is particularly pronounced in Hinduism: coconut and mango represent the sacred and auspicious; ghee (clarified butter) indicates purity; rice and bananas are symbols of fertility.

The calendar of feasting is balanced in many cultures by one of fasting. Sometimes there is a regular fast every week. In the Eastern Orthodox church, for example, Wednesday and Friday are the traditional days of fasting. Some religions also have annual

fasts. A well known example is Ramadan, the period of restraint during which Muslims fast from dawn to sunset for 30 days. Such major fasts are usually themselves ended by a feast. The Muslim festival of Eid ul-Fitr, which begins with a good breakfast, and continues with the eating of sweets such as sugared almonds, marks the end of Ramadan.

In some cultures the fasting follows the feasting. For example, the Christian period of abstinence, Lent, is traditionally preceded by carnival (the word dervies from the Latin for 'farewell to meat'). Festivals, parades, and feasting take place during the weeks or days leading up to Shrove Tuesday, thc day before

SALT
For thousands of years people have enjoyed the taste of salt on their food and have valued it as a food preservative. Some of the world's oldest roads are the ancient salt routes, along which the precious cargo was carried. In the Middle Ages, one's social standing could be gauged by where one sat in relation to the salt cellar in the castle hall. To sit 'above the salt' on the daïs was an indication of high status; lesser mortals sat 'below the salt'. In southern Ethiopia the bride price paid by the groom's family to that of the bride is often paid in salt.

IN THE SALT MINES
Salt miners have made sculptures in salt for thousands of years. Some of the most magnificent salt carvings are in the vast chambers in the Wieliczka mine in Poland. Here, there is even a chapel with altar candlesticks and statues all carved out of salt.

the beginning of Lent. In New Orleans, this day is referred to as Mardi Gras – fat Tuesday – an allusion to the fact that all the fat stored throughout the winter was to be used up before Lent. From Venice to Rio, this is a time during which Christian communities let their hair down.

FOOD AND SOCIAL STATUS

What we eat often says something about our social status. People who can afford expensive foods have a higher status than those who survive on staples. Frequently, the value attached to a particular food is related to its rarity. In a hunter-gatherer society, for example, it is likely to be the meat of an animal that is scarce or difficult to track down that attracts prestige. In Elizabethan England luxury foods were those made from commodities that had to be imported. Sugar, for example, was a costly luxury and foods sweetened with it were accessible only to the rich. The connection between food and wealth may be even closer. The Fulani of Nigeria, like the ancient Irish, Germans and Greeks, measure wealth in terms of cattle ownership. A Fulani farmer is therefore unwilling to slaughter cattle, and the eating of beef is mainly confined to feast days.

Sometimes there is a reversal of status. In the early days of farming, all flour was unrefined and bread was brown or black. But as grinding and milling techniques advanced, white bread started to appear, made from flour from which a large proportion of the fibre had been removed. At first, the white bread conferred great status on the eater. But nowadays, with white bread easy to obtain, the prestige, in northern countries at least, has transferred to the coarser wholemeal breads.

Such changes reflect the fashion element in food. This is particularly noticeable in the West, where the power of advertising and the media can bring a particular food rapidly into

THE MYSTERIOUS TRUFFLE

The Périgord region of southern France and parts of central Italy are some of the best-known truffle-growing areas. These wild fungi have become typical luxury foods – they grow only in certain restricted areas, they are difficult to locate, and seem impossible to cultivate commercially. This mystique, together with their distinctive flavour, makes them especially prized by gastronomes.

Truffle-hunting is a familiar rural pursuit in the places where the fungi grow. Truffle-hunters have long realized that they need help in finding these delicacies. Sometimes a dog is used, but the traditional partner of the truffle-hunter is a specially trained pig. The hunter often carries a stick to keep the pig away from the truffles when they are finally found.

TRUFFLE-HUNTERS
Some old hands go truffle-hunting, without the help of a dog or a pig, using their knowledge of where to look. Truffles are most commonly found near the roots of trees, especially beech and oak.

BEER FESTIVALS

From the pale lagers of the Czech Republic and Germany to the dark brown bitter brews of England, beer has long been a traditional drink in northern Europe. Hops grow well in the cooler northern climates where vines are less easy to cultivate. Beer festivals began as celebrations of the hop harvest, festivities that signalled pleasure that there would be a year's good drinking – and a year's good profits for the brewer. But the larger festivals, such as the Oktoberfest in Munich and the Bockbier Festival in Berlin have taken on a life of their own. They are carnival-like times of licence and good living, when the conoisseur can sample different brews – and others can get drunk. The beer is traditionally served in earthenware mugs, and white radishes are eaten to stimulate the thirst.

THE PLOUGHMAN'S LUNCH
Bread, cheese, pickled onions, and perhaps a little salad: the ploughman's lunch forms a standard accompaniment to beer in many British public houses. It has become so common that it is already thought of as traditional, even though it was invented by mid 20th-century pub-owners looking for an easy-to-prepare meal.

the public eye and where technological advances can make a once scarce food cheap and easy to obtain.

The company with whom we share our food also reflects our social position. Hindu Brahmins do not eat with untouchables. In the Middle Ages, in the castles and great houses of Europe, the lord and his family sat at a high table 'above' the salt cellar, while the lower classes sat below. Nowadays, it is still traditional in many families for the head of the household to sit at the 'head of the table', while at formal meals the chief guest will be seated next to the host, with other guests arrayed on either side in a descending hierarchy of importance. At the older universities in England, many colleges still have 'high tables', at which teaching staff and their guests, but not (normally) undergraduates, eat. Many colleges also insist that academic gowns be worn at dinner – at least at high table.

Factories often have one dining room for 'workers', another for management or directors. The Chinese sometimes have a tussle about who should sit where or even who sould go into the dining room first: to westerners it may look like rudeness, but in fact it is elaborate politeness. Wherever there is a social hierarchy, such systems operate.

Like the religious food customs, these customs work in two ways. They exclude some people from the table, but strengthen the group that is admitted to dine. Food is thus an important element in friendship, togetherness, and communication between people with other things in common. Hospitality is traditionally a highly regarded virtue for this reason.

Eating, then, provides one of our richest social indicators. Food can tell much about our environment and the economic basis of a society: it can reflect the habits and customs of millenia; it can symbolize social position; it can can embody timeless symbols. In nurturing the body we give the mind food for thought and provide a rich diet for the spirit.

Healing

Modern medicine has transformed the world. From the newest hospital in the United States to the most basic clinic in an African village, doctors and nurses trained in western medicine are making incredible strides towards the eradication of disease through such means as immunization, advances in hygiene, the development of new treatments.

But there are many systems of medicine operating in the world, some with traditions of healing stretching back thousands of years, some with millions of satisfied patients in their care. These systems are very varied. They range from acupuncture, with its use of needles that are held to affect the flow of energy through the body, to the shamanic practices of people living traditional lifestyles.

These diverse systems of medicine have more in common than at first seems to be the case. Above all they are holistic: they consider the patient as a whole person, often concerning themselves as much with the patient's mental and spiritual well-being as with their bodily health. This is in contrast to western medicine's concentration on specific symptoms with the aim of arriving at a precise diagnosis that defines the parts of the person's body that need to be treated. The importance attached to the spiritual health in traditional medicine often goes together with a strong ritual element.

THE WORLD OF THE SPIRIT

For many peoples, the spirit comes first. The world of the spirit is real and powerful. Illnesses are often held to be the result of the influence of spirits that are discontented with the behaviour of humans. The first step is to communicate with the malign spirit (either to appease it or to gain more knowledge of the

nature of the disease), and this can be done with the help of ceremonies and rituals.

Much of the work of the shaman – the priest, witch-doctor or medicine man of traditional religions – is concerned with getting closer to the sacred realities that are beyond the experience of most people. From such a standpoint, the shaman can achieve new perspectives on the world, together with new perceptions, visions of the future, and the power of healing. So shamans speak of passing 'from one world to another'.

To do this they may wear costumes that conjure up the presence of mythical creatures or gods. Thus Japanese shamans wore hats of owl and eagle feathers and cloaks decorated with stuffed snakes. Other shamans wear costumes that depict creatures of power such as bears and wild cats.

The use of music, dance and drumming is another important way in which the shaman maintains contact with the spirit world. The spiritual forces are invoked by means of words and movements that have been handed down from one generation to the next Perhaps the most widespread feature is the use of the drum, an almost universal musical instrument. It does more than dictate the rhythm of the dance. Many shamans speak of the drum as opening up a path between the human and spirit worlds.

THE SPIRITS AND HEALING

The traditional Apache response to some illnesses is one example of how the spirit and human worlds are considered to interact. The

THE WORLD OF THE SPIRIT HEALER
In traditional societies, healing rituals often involve making contact with the spirit world. The shaman achieves this with the help of music, drumming and the wearing of special masks and costumes.

THE MASK OF THE SHAMAN

Masks and costumes are often used in healing ceremonies performed by shamans. They work in two apparently opposite ways. They help the wearer to impersonate another being, human or spiritual; but they also conceal the wearer's true identity. This works well for the shaman: he has to summon up spirits; he has to act as the representative of the spirit world on Earth, and may want to play down his own personality in doing this.

TLINGIT MASK

The astonished expression of this Tlingit mask from the northwestern American coast reminds those who look at it of the dangers of the medicine man's spirit journey, dangers that are repeated at each ceremony in which he takes part.

Apache and other native North American peoples have a pronounced fear of coming into contact with the dead, or even looking at dead bodies. This fear extends to owls, because they believe that ghosts appear in the form of these nocturnal birds. Illnesses are sometimes said to be the result of seeing an owl, and are referred to as 'owl sickness' or 'ghost sickness'. A shaman may be asked to come and sing over someone suffering from owl sickness. The song will help the shaman determine the cause of the disorder.

The shamans of the Sioux people of North America use song in a similar way. The writer Arthur Versluis recounts the story of a contemporary healing performed by the Sioux shaman Wallace Black Elk. Conventional doctors had failed to treat a young boy, who could neither speak nor move. The shaman came to the boy's hospital room, shut the curtains to make it completely dark, and sang ritual songs. Wallace Black Elk recalled that a figure called Tunkashila, an embodiment of God in the shape of a glowing man, appeared, and told the shaman that the boy had been attacked in a way that used the force of a spider's web that was lodged in his brain. Wallace Black Elk then summoned the red spider spirit, who came and removed the web. The boy was cured.

The traditional healer often has a collection of ritual objects that help to make contact with the spirit world. In southern Africa, for example, healers ritually twirl a horse's mane to ward off evil spirits before a consultation begins. The healer also carries a bag full of small objects that may be used in diagnosis. These objects, which may include anything from animal teeth and shells to beads and dice, are thrown in the air, and a diagnosis or prediction is made according to which way up they land. Their position also helps the healer

SIBERIAN COSTUME
A mask can be extended into a costume that covers the entire body. This Siberian shaman's costume allows the wearer to conceal himself behind a host of symbols. They include images of spirits, a mirror to help him see into other world, and ribbons called wings that indicate the shaman's ability to fly.

HORNED HEADDRESS, UTAH
The horns remind one of the fertility of the natural world and the power to which the shaman has access.

to prescribe a variety of treatments, from herbal medicines to ritual bathing. The healer's ritual equipment is often revered – so much so that in some Nigerian communities it is kept in a special house that only a shaman is allowed to enter.

Often the shaman finds it necessary to send a spirit away from a sick person. There are many ways of doing this. In northwestern Australia, a shaman may suck the spirit out of the patient's body, carry it away in his hands and bury it. In some Melanesian islands, the tradition is to attach some charmed material inhabited by the spirit to an arrow and to shoot the spirit as far away as possible. Another method, once common in Africa, involved transferring the spirit to an animal, which was then slaughtered thereby curing the disease. Such a ritual is similar to the tradition of the 'scapegoat', a figure representing death that was ritually destroyed in some German carnival and Easter celebrations.

Close contact with the world of the spirits is not confined to people living traditional lifestyles. The phenomenon of the Christian spiritual healer is well known. According to

the gospels, Christ himself healed the sick, indeed raised the dead, and some Christian ministers still hold healing services, combining Christian prayer with specific healing rites.

In medieval Europe, when kings were attributed divine qualities, monarchs were often said to have a healing touch. One of the most familiar examples of this was the ruler's alleged power to cure scrofula (tuberculosis of the lymphatic glands). So closely was this disorder linked to the healing abilities of monarchs that it was known as the 'king's evil'.

Today, people in the West, educated in the scientific tradition to reject the inexplicable, often look upon such accounts with scepticism. But Christian healers have much in common with their counterparts in traditional societies. Many healing rituals use the power of human touch, the 'laying on of hands', and some healers use a mixture of Christian and non-Christian rites. The Peruvian healer Eduardo Calderón, for example, invoked both his shamanistic predecessors and the Christian saints when beginning a healing session.

QUESTIONS OF BALANCE

Many systems of medicine describe body function in terms of balance. In Chinese medicine, for example, it is important to balance *yin* and *yang;* Indian Ayurvedic medicine aims to balance 'hot' and 'cold' elements.

These states of balance may be restored in many different ways. A Chinese doctor may use acupuncture in the belief that a person's health is influenced by the flow of a vital energy force known as *chi* or *qi* along lines, called meridians, that run up and down the body. The insertion of a needle at certain points in the meridians is held to affect the flow of *qi* and thereby restore balance to the body.

Needles are not the Chinese doctor's only resource. Herbal medicines may also be prescribed, and these are chosen and made up according to a vast pharmacopoeia of medicinal

Healing plants

Herbalists today use plants from many different healing traditions, sometimes even combining herbs from Europe, America, and the Far East. Some of the common names of these plants reflect their traditional uses.

Figwort
The Latin name of this plant, *Scrophularia nodosa*, reveals that it was once used in the treatment of the disease scrofula (king's evil), a form of tuberculosis. Nowadays it is more likely to be used to treat skin diseases.

Motherwort
This plant was given to women after childbirth. Its Latin name, *Leonurus cardiaca*, also reveals that it was used to treat palpitations.

Pasque flower
This herb was traditionally gathered at Easter, when it is in flower. The English name of pasque flower, *Anemone pulsatilla*, comes from an Old French word for Easter. The stems of the plant were used for disorders of the reproductive system.

Eyebright
A traditional English remedy, eyebright (*Euphrasia officinalis*) is best known among herbalists for its beneficial effect in diseases of the eye. It is also used to treat sinusitis and nasal catarrh.

Ginger
Familiar as a culinary herb, ginger (*Zingiber officinale*) is used by both western and Chinese herbalists. In the West it is used to relieve indigestion. In both traditions it is used to treat colds and flu, although the Chinese distinguish between fresh ginger (for colds) and dried ginger (for other respiratory and digestive problems).

Comfrey
The roots and leaves of comfrey (*Symphytum officinale*) are used by herbalists in the treatment of a wide range of disorders, including gastric ulcers and coughs, and to speed the healing of wounds

plants, many of which have been used for thousands of years. These plants include many that are familiar because of their culinary uses. The fact that these plants are used in cooking as well as medicine is important; both food and medicine have a role in fostering good health.

The maintainance of balance is crucial, then, to both Chinese physician and Chinese cook. Indeed, there was a tradition in China that the doctor was employed on a regular basis to ensure that the balance was maintained – you did not simply consult the physician when you were ill. Furthermore, you paid the doctor only when you were well; if you had an illness, payments were withheld until the balance of *yin* and *yang* was restored.

Green medicine

Healing has always looked to the earth. Ancient people soothed their stomachs with clay. It quelled the pangs of hunger, and is still sometimes eaten in places as far afield as West Africa and South Carolina. But the first true medicines were probably herbs and for thousands of years herbal medicine was all that was available.

Over the generations, knowledge of the healing properties of local plants was gathered and gradually became more and more specific. Particular species would be prescribed for individual ailments. People devised ways of remembering their effects. So the common name of a plant would reflect its medicinal uses – for example, self heal, woundwort, eyebright.

Still later, such lore was codified into what amounted almost to dogma. The so-called 'doctrine of signatures' suggested that like always cured like – in other words a plant that in some way resembled an ailment or part of the body should be used to cure that disease or organ. For example, it was said that a plant with kidney-shaped leaves helped the kidneys.

Other customs were associated with the use of herbs. There were elaborate conventions

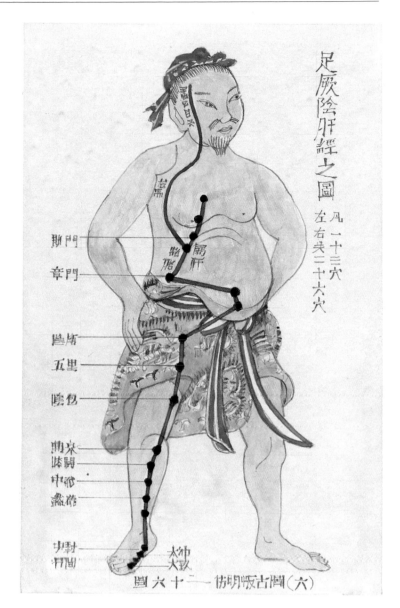

ACUPUNCTURE
Chinese physicians believe that *qi* flows through the body along a network of pathways known as meridians. One meridian is shown here.

about when the plants should be harvested. These rules did not simply cover the time of year, but even the time of day or phase of the moon when it was best to gather the leaves or roots used in medicine. Often the timing had obvious reasons. Roots, for example, were gathered at the end of the growing season, the point at which they contain the most nutrients.

Women's work?

In an age before widespread travel, herbal medicine relied on the plants that were available locally. It also relied on local practitioners, often women, who built up a

THE POWER OF TOUCH
Many healers from widely differing traditions make use of the power of touch. In some cases it is as if a health-giving power is communicated through the fingers. Sometimes science can explain this effect. In other cases it is a mystery more related to the world of the spirit than to the physical world of science.

HOLISTIC MASSAGE
In this type of massage, the entire body is treated. At the end, the masseur will make long 'connecting' strokes, to reaffirm a sense of the person's wholeness after the inidividual parts of the body have been massaged.

REFLEXOLOGY
Although reflexologists work only on the feet, the therapy is considered holistic, since the pressure points on the feet are said to affect the energy flow to all parts of the body.

OSTEOPATHY
An osteopath manipulates and re-aligns the joints, based on a thorough knowledge of the human musculo-skeletal system.

CHRISTIAN FAITH-HEALER
The laying-on of hands is a familiar part of Christian healing rituals. Faith in the effectiveness of the process is necessary for the healing to work.

WORKING ON THE AURA
There are healers who treat disease by working on the person's aura (the invisible nimbus surrounding the body) without actually touching the patient's body.

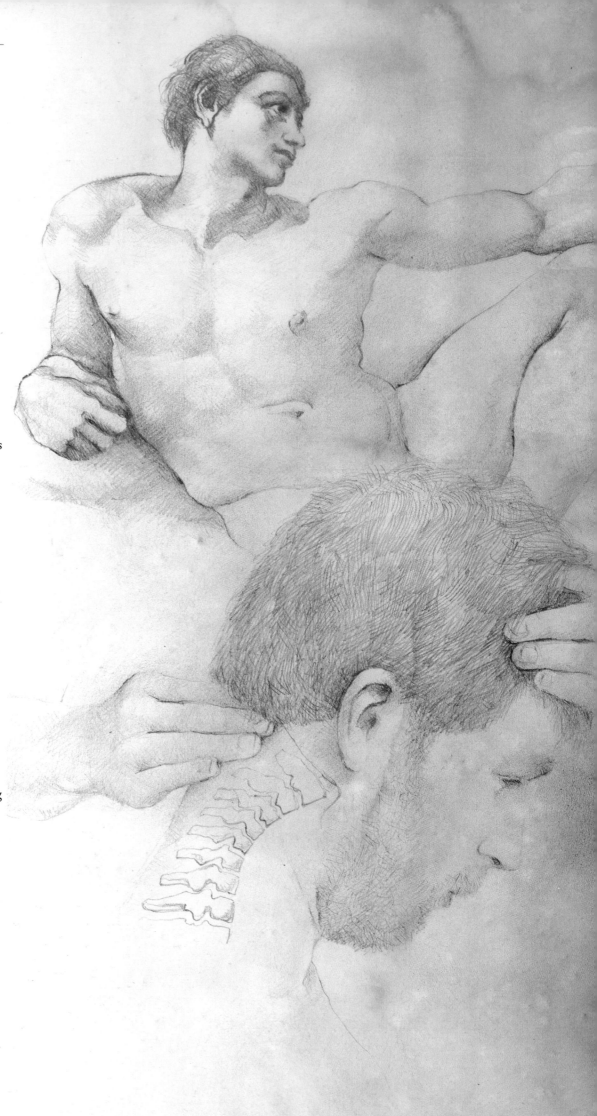

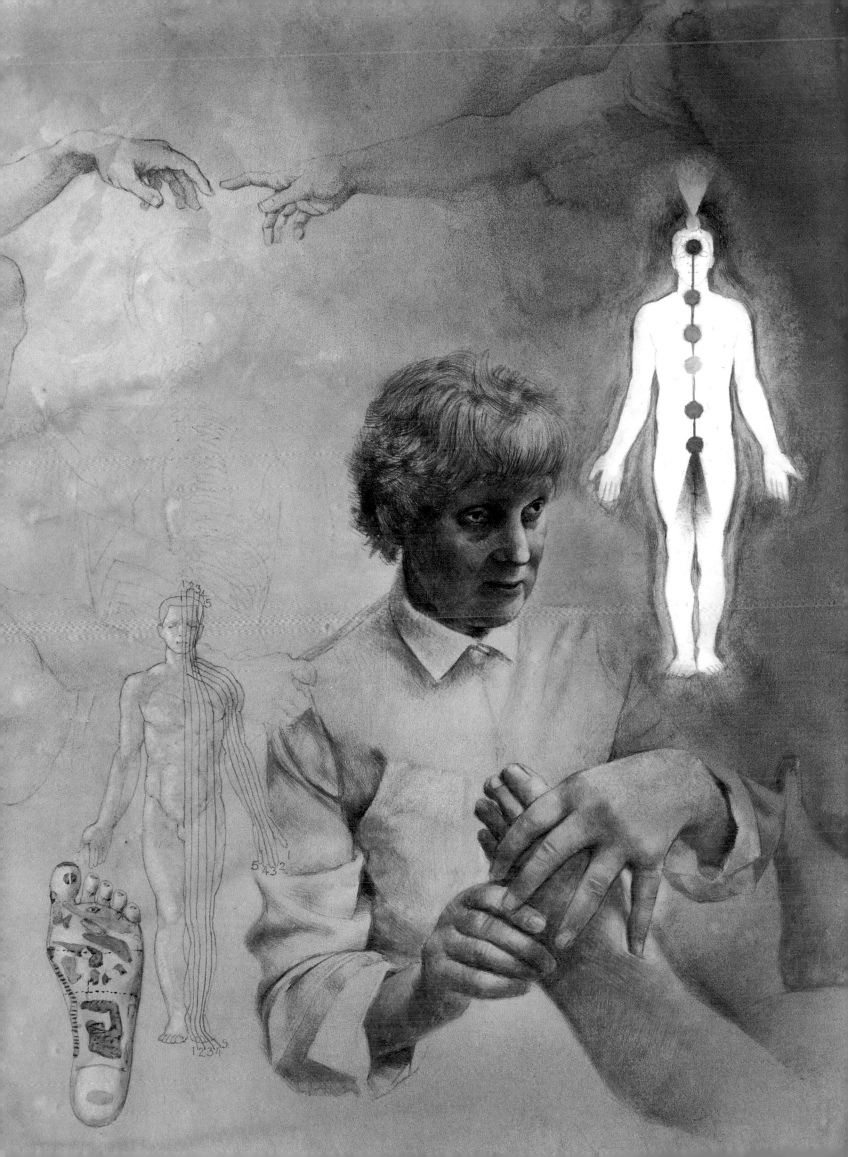

large body of knowledge about healing plants and passed it down through the generations. Valued as it was by the patients, the wisdom of such women was viewed with suspicion by medieval western churchmen. 'Wise women', whose only crime was a knowledge of the power of plants, even risked being persecuted as witches. Knowledge of medicinal herbs was also kept alive in the monasteries, but individuals who had no access to the infirmaries run by the church had to prescribe what cures they could at home. Without formal training but with the benefit of generations of accumulated traditional knowledge, women all over the world carried on treating common ailments with herbs.

MODERN RITUALS

While based on the so-called objective tenets of science, western medicine is just as ritualized as any of its traditional counterparts. Its rigid hierarchies and divisions between physicians and nurses, its costumes, the regular patterns of life in the hospital ward and the rigorous routines of the operating theatre, all these involve the sort of repeated actions that we call rituals. Perhaps the tradition of the ward round, in which the senior physician, with full entourage of junior doctors and students, briefly visits each patient, holds forth on their condition, questions the students and then passes magesterially on, is the most formal, and, for many, the most forbidding of all these ceremonies.

Where human health is concerned, where it might be a question of life or death, it is vital to follow the correct methods. Whatever the system of medicine, whatever the condition of the patient, there are set routines to follow, procedures to be followed. This is obviously true when one is undergoing treatment with a native American shaman or going for a therapeutic massage by an expert in the Japanese technique of Shiatsu. Every form of

medicine, it might be said, has its rituals, from the judicious, probing questions the patient is subjected to in disciplines as diverse as psychoanalysis and homeopathy to the careful physical examination and manipulation that an osteopath's patient undergoes. But it is equally the case if one is being admitted to a modern hospital – filling in forms, being examined by a physician and perhaps by medical students and attended by a nurse.

The effect in all such cases is that the patient surrenders to the expertise of the healer Whether you call it trust or faith, modern studies seem to confirm that such rituals are beneficial to the patient. Trials have shown, for example, that counselling is often as important in western medicine as the prescription of drugs. Indeed, the two work hand-in-hand: researchers have found that drugs are more likely to work if there is also counselling, when the physician and the patient discuss the disease and its treatment.

LEARNING THE CRAFT

Training is as important for the shaman as for any western physician. An early 20th-century account of the training of a South American shaman describes how this begins when the candidate is quite young. First, the young man must show that he is mentally strong enough to deal with the spirit world. So he spends long periods living alone in an isolated place. He must endure extended periods of fasting and must practise silence and abstinence. He must take strong emetics and must undertake combats, real or symbolic, with wild beasts.

The ritual training of the shaman can be directly related to his healing role. It often involves a 'spirit vision' in which the initiate encounters a guiding spirit and previews some of the visions or rituals in which he will take part in the future. A native North American shaman, for example, described a vision in which a bear danced. The creature ripped open his belly and healed himself; then two bears tore at each other's flesh and, once more, healed themselves. On each occasion the bears 'made themselves holy' before the healing, prefiguring the ritual the shaman will have to go through before each healing session.

The Yakut people of Siberia explain the power of the shaman according to his spirit vision. The young trainee shaman is handed over to dreadful spirits who, it is said, hack his flesh to pieces. The spirits eat parts of the shaman's body, and the diseases that the shaman will be able to treat depend on the parts eaten by the spirit. So if the spirits eat part of the shaman's belly, he will be able to cure stomach illnesses, and so on.

The young shaman must also learn the lore of his craft. Typically, an older, fully trained shaman accompanies him and teaches him about the properties and uses of medicinal plants, about the sorts of ceremonies he will have to perform, and about the dances he will be expected to dance and the music he will use in his rituals. In some parts of South America, the shaman learns how to perform apparently magical acts, during which in a haze of tobacco smoke, he apparently extracts all manner of items, from stones to insects, from the diseased parts of peoples' bodies.

The power of the traditional shaman, even when apparently performing sophisticated trickery, can be enormous. It reminds us of the importance of ritual in all systems of medicine, and how this can sometimes be of key importance in triggering the healing process, helping the body to cure itself.

HEALING SYMBOLS
As well as relying on the healing powers of herbs or medicines, healers from different cultures draw on a rich cultural heritage, often represented by religious symbols. From top to bottom, these examples are the Chinese symbol of *yin* and *yang,* the two essential qualities that must be held in balance; AUM, the Hindu sacred syllable, the essence of all sounds; ankh, the ancient Egyptian sign of life, which seems to prefigure the Christian cross; and a further version of AUM.

SOCIALIZING

FROM JOINING GROUPS TO
SETTLING DISPUTES:
MAKING AND MAINTAINING SOCIAL TIES

The ability to organize ourselves into groups for a common aim has produced some of our most impressive achievements, from the pyramids to the United Nations. Social groups, from the school to the workplace, the family to the tribe or state, are all around us. Most of us belong to several such groups. And many groups use ritual to increase the sense of belonging.

Forging links

Among the clearest examples of this are initiation ceremonies, the rituals performed when new members join a group. In some cultures these rituals are indistinguishable from the ceremonies performed when an individual comes of age (see pages 60-75). But there are many organizations – groups as diverse as the Freemasons and the priesthood – that are not necessarily entered at this time of life, and they frequently have special initiation rites. Such ceremonies, designed to ensure that a new person joins the group on the right footing, introduce the new member, outline rules and prescribe appropriate behaviour. The ritual may also include tests to discover if the person is fit to belong to the group.

Maintaining links

If initiations are about beginnings, there are also customs and rituals concerned with continuity and with keeping the ties of society secure. Gift-giving ceremonies often fall into this category. This can be as true when nations give gifts to nations as when an individual is given a birthday present: the Statue of Liberty, a gift from France to the United States, is a permanent reminder of the link between two nations. All gift-giving is an exercise in communication, in keeping the channels open, even for those who exchange gifts only at birthdays or Christmas.

What happens if, in spite of the bonds that have been set up, these links break down? Societies have a whole range of ritualized mechanisms to resolve disputes. The rituals and formal procedures allow opposing sides to present their cases without coming to blows, and to provide the forum for a judgement that will be respected by all parties. Sometimes the confrontation between the parties in a dispute is ritualized, as in places where a ritual wrestling match or an entertaining singing contest can be used to decide the case. Perhaps the most effective rituals of social belonging make it fun to belong. Whether they are revealing the mysteries of a secret society to a new initiate, enabling us to exchange gifts, or helping us to resolve our differences with an operatic flourish, such rituals emphasize how enjoyable it can be to be part of 'the family of man'.

Initiation

Earlier in this book we have seen how ceremonies are used to mark a person's passage from one stage of life to another. These rites of passage are the great universal ceremonies, which are celebrated all over the world.

But there are other rituals, less widespread but equally important where they occur, that mark different human journeys. Often these are passages into a new social group, into a society of people with a common interest, a religious order, a school, or a new place of work. The rites that mark these different passages are themselves varied, but they are all beginnings, rites of entry into a new social grouping. For this reason it seems right to call them initiation ceremonies.

BECOMING ACCEPTED

In a short story by the American writer Dashiell Hammett, a private investigator is hired as deputy sheriff in a rough settlement in Arizona. His first job on arriving in town is to buy himself a horse, and a group of ruffians take him to a ranch where a suitable animal is said to be for sale. The deputy, a city man and no great rider, sits astride the animal and his worst fears are confirmed: the beast is unbroken and rapidly throws him on the ground. Not to be defeated, and knowing what will happen, the deputy remounts and is thrown three times more. By this time the men who brought him to the ranch are begging him to stop. He has earned their respect.

Joining a new social group is often rather like this. One has to prove one's mettle, and a special ordeal is frequently provided. In the genteel surroundings of English public schools and the older universities, the initiation can be almost as barbaric as in Hammett's fictional

DEDICATION
In many cultures, the first haircut is a significant step in growing up. Shaving the head may also be a prelude to a period of study with a spiritual master.

American West. In more than one school, a newcomer is welcomed by the older pupils by having his head dunked in a lavatory pan. And in some Oxford colleges, freshmen were initiated by being made to drink an enormous tankard of beer at a single gulp.

Of course there are also more decorous official ceremonies for those entering school or university. These include the elaborate gowned matriculation ceremonies sometimes seen in the older universities. Such rituals sometimes contain useful instruction, giving the newcomer information about how to get on in a strange new world. But just as often they are simple welcomes.

STARTING SCHOOL

Perhaps the first major life-change most people experience is when they start school. For probably the first time, the small child has to cope with a new social group, a new place and a new discipline. All this can be a shock to the system, but it also marks the beginning of new discoveries and new friendships.

COURAGE!

Traditionally, Jewish children were given a spoonful of honey before being sent to school for the first time. The sweet-tasting treat gave them some compensation for the anxiety. It was also meant to suggest, in a society where scholarship is revered, that learning is sweet.

WELCOME!

Children on their first day at kindergarten in Japan dress in their best clothes for a welcoming ceremony, designed both to reassure them and to instill a sense of the importance of school. The culmination is a group photograph of the new pupils.

As with beginnings, so with endings. Gaining a college degree, is in one way an ending, but is also the beginning of a new stage of one's life. There are similar ceremonies at all levels of qualification. Lawyers may be welcomed to the bar with a ceremonial dinner; newly qualified army officers attend a passing out parade; those who have completed a craft apprenticeship have their own special rituals. And every nation has a special ceremony for confirming the office of a new head of state.

HONOURS AND OATHS

Many societies have special ways of honouring those who have given special service or who stand out in some way. The granting of an order or medal, or the giving of a special prize, is usually marked with a special ceremony. Some of these rituals date back hundreds of years. In the British ceremony for awarding a knighthood, for example, the candidate kneels in front of the monarch, who touches his shoulders with the flat of a sword blade, before bidding the new knight to rise. This ritual dates back to medieval dubbings, which were usually the culmination of years of training, during which a youth would rise in rank from page to squire before being granted the status of knighthood.

Other contemporary honours may be marked in a more modern way – for example, with a handshake or the handing over of special insignia. Or the recipient of the honour may stand to attention while a medal is pinned on to his or her coat.

Frequently an initiation involves a 'two-way traffic', in which a new status is granted on certain conditions. A new member of a parliament may take his or her seat in a formal

MASONIC INITIATION
In a secret rite involving blindfolding and the use of masonic emblems, a new recruit is initiated into the craft of Freemasonry.

ceremony. In return, he or she will probably have to swear an oath of allegiance, agreeing to serve the institution faithfully and to abide by the constitution.

SECRETS REVEALED

The initiation ritual may well emphasize the exclusivity of the society in question, while opening up secrets to the newcomer. In most places there are societies like this, ranging from the secret societies of traditional cultures to associations like that of the Freemasons, which has considerable influence in the West.

A man who is about to become a Freemason is entrusted with knowledge of a number of secret signs, passwords and

handshakes with which he and fellow masons will be able to make themselves known to each other. He also takes part in an elaborate ritual drama of initiation. This ritual, the details of which are concealed from ousiders, involves the initiate in a blindfolded ceremonial journey. He is asked questions and is expected to answer according to a set formula – it is vital to get the words exactly right. He undergoes certain ordeals that may be accompanied by bewildering noises as members bang together squares, compasses, and other masonic symbols. Finally, at the words 'Let there be light', the blindfold is removed and he is admitted to the rank of Masonic apprentice, given his apron of white lambskin and white gloves, and introduced to the other members of the Lodge. Further initiation rituals are performed as the member moves from apprenticeship through the other degrees of the craft.

This ritual indicates to the participants that the initiate has begun a new life. The ceremony removed him from his old context, took him

SPECIAL COSTUMES
An initiate may be asked to wear special clothes, including garments that refer back to the imperial past of the culture.

on his symbolic journey to the inner sanctum of the Lodge, gave him his new identity, and welcomed him into the new society. The rituals of Freemasonry have their own special flavour, which derives from the western Christian tradition in which the craft grew up. Much of the symbolism of Freemasonry – squares, compasses and other paraphenalia of the stone mason – derives from its association with Hiram Abiff, reputed architect of King Solomon's temple.

The symbolism of Chinese secret societies

EMERGING POWER
During some traditional Mexican initiations, the priest appears, as if by magic, from a pit in the floor.

like the Triad is very different. The place where the ceremonies are performed is referred to as a walled city, a palace or a temple. The inner courtyard is known as the Red Flower Pavilion. The officials wear robes of a Ming dynasty design – clearly an allusion to the origins of the society in imperial China. There is also much Buddhist symbolism, reflecting the fact that certain Triad societies, such as the important White Lotus society, are said to have been formed to meditate on the name of Buddha and on the Buddhist way of life.

But in other ways the Triad and Masonic rituals are rather similar. There is also a ritual

journey into an inner sanctum. There are challenges and questions to be answered. There are secrets to be divulged, and oaths of secrecy to be taken. The initiates are admitted to a new brotherhood to which they must remain loyal. As with the rituals, so with the societies: both offer their members exclusivity (not anyone can be a member) and fraternity (masons say that the shared meals and charitable works are more important than the rituals).

TRADITIONAL SECRET SOCIETIES

Organizations such as the Triad and the Freemasons operate mainly in modern, industrialized societies. But many traditional societies also have secret groups that offer similar benefits to their members, as well as playing an important role in the larger societies of which they form a part. Often initiation into these secret groups takes place at the same time as the person is initiated into adulthood.

The Hopi Pueblo people of Arizona and New Mexico, for example, have four societies for men (two concerned with fertility, two with defensive magic and death), and three societies for women. The societies perform

WISDOM OF THE FOREST
In many rural communities, initiation is performed by someone with knowledge of the local environment.

rites in *kivas*, underground chambers with a raised southern area and a sunken northern part with a fire, stone benches, an altar and a cavity in the middle of the floor. The rituals take place in this northern part of the *kiva*.

One Hopi initiaton ceremony includes a drama of the creation. According to the Hopi creation myth, the first people climbed to Earth from the underworld through a hole in the ground. They were accompanied by spirits, who had to return to the underworld. The floor cavity in the *kiva* represents a hole through which the first Hopi climbed from the underworld. In the initiation ritual, masked men portray the spirits, who are also identified with the dead. They show the young people being initiated how the Hopi dead are born into the underworld, just as children are born into the upper world. Initiation is vital because only through this ceremony will the children be able to gain their own place in the underworld when the time comes for them to join the dead.

The image of rebirth is quite common in initiation ceremonies. Some of the peoples of the lower Congo in Africa, had a ceremony in which a number of initiates would ceremonially 'die'. They would then be carried to an enclosure some distance from the village, where they would remain for several months. During this time the chief would teach them the ways of a secret society, including a secret language, and give them new names. While they were away, those left behind in the village would say that the bodies of the initiates had decayed to a single bone, which the chief brought back to life.

RELIGIOUS INITIATION

The initiation ceremony is not just a prelude to adulthood, not merely an entry to a new type of society, but a key stage in an individual's development. In many religions, the ceremony of entry to the faith fulfils this function.

NEW JOB, NEW SOCIAL STATUS

People who are taking up a post in public life usually undergo an elaborate public initiation. Coronations in the West, like that of the British queen in 1953, are well known. But all societies have ceremonies that publicize the appointments of new rulers or officials and confirm the power of the new office-holder.

CORONATION

Queen Elizabeth II was crowned in one of her country's great churches, Westminster Abbey. A complex and highly theatrical series of ceremonies took place. Each ceremony had its own significance. The recognition, when the Archbishop presiding announced 'I here present unto you Queen Elizabeth, your undoubted Queen...' made the monarch's identity clear and allowed the assembled people the chance to express their loyalty.

A ceremony of anointing embraced the ruler's spiritual role, supposedly imbuing her with spiritual grace. The presenting of the sword called forth her temporal power and role as military leader. The crowning and enthroning provided a fitting climax to the whole ceremony, when the monarch was also given the Sceptre with the Cross, symbolizing power and justice, and the Rod with the Dove, representing equality and mercy.

Confirmation, for example, is seen as a vital rite in many branches of the Christian church. While once it was a matter of course for children growing up in a Christian community to be confirmed, with confirmation playing the role of a rite of passage into adolescence, now it is a clear signal that the individual has made the choice to become a Christian, preceded by preparatory classes and culminating in a ceremony of entry to the church.

Other religions allow devotees to enter temporarily a state that will enhance spiritual well-being. This is the role played by Buddhist monkhood for many young men in Thailand. They are not expected to remain monks for life; most stay at the monastery for only a few months. But this period of monkhood is seen as an important experience that brings merit to a young man and his family before he settles down to married life. The ordination ceremony is laid down precisely in the classical Buddhist texts, but many local variations exist.

The candidate for monkhood starts by spending seven days at the temple, during which he is to learn the the words of the rite that he will soon attend. On the day before the actual ordination, his friends and relatives bring the eight items that he will need: two robes, an umbrella, a bowl, a pair of slippers, a lamp, a razor and a begging bowl. The monk has his head shaved. Later on this same day the men who are be ordained gather together and perform a ceremony with the village elders. Part of this ceremony involves 'calling the *khwan*' (spirit-essence), during which the spirit-essence is said to enter the young man's body. He is reminded that in becoming a monk he is fulfilling a duty to his parents.

On the day of the ordination there is a procession to the temple, with the young man carried on a palanquin and attended by two teacher-monks. At the temple, the man performs obeisances to his father and the attendant monks (there must be at least five monks present for the ordination to take place), and asks for permission to be ordained. After responding to certain questions, the young man is declared a novice. Gifts are given to the monk who presides over the ceremony. Further questions are levelled at the novice, to find out whether he is a suitable candidate for full monkhood. He is also told about the rules he must obey and given a homily about the qualities of a monk. Chanting and a blessing follow, during which the new monk pours water, indicating the transference of merit to his relatives. Finally, there is a feast for the monks, relatives and villagers.

This complex ceremony has many functions. It instructs and assesses the new monk; it ensures that he has the equipment he needs; it involves parents, relatives and the

ATONEMENT
Tibetan Buddhists have a ritual called Nyungne, a period of atonement and abstention from sex, conversation, work, and for part of the time from food and drink. Except at the end of the four-day ritual, there is silence in

whole village in the man's change of status; it transfers merit to the parents as well as to the monk himself. It highlights how initiation ceremonies, like many rites of passage can be as much for the benefit of the rest of society as for the individuals who are actually passing from one stage to another.

LIFE'S JOURNEYS

The beginning of a new stage in life is often seen as a journey. A literal journey is also often surrounded with ritual. Formal farewells are in order when someone is going far away or is leaving for a long time. Journeys themselves often have a special significance and the idea of the pilgrimage is common to many religions:

Muslims travel to Mecca, Hindus to the Ganges and other sites, Christians to a host of holy places. Such pilgrimages are often turning points, marking the transition from one stage in a person's life to another. The journey to Mecca is the high point of the life of any Muslim. Christians have reported miraculuous life changes as a result of pilgrimages. Hindus believe that the waters of the Ganges can counterthe effects of bad deeds

Many religions see the funeral rites as the ultimate initiation, into the next life. The close connection between death and renewal is a theme that is present in all sorts of initiations, which are frequently as important and life-enhancing for the spectators in the audience as for the participants who hold centre stage.

the temple and children are excluded, because it is feared that they will not stay quiet. The observance of Nyungne is voluntary and brings merit to the individual. This is important to Buddhists, because the more merit in proportion to sin one has accrued during life, the better one's state on rebirth.

THE FOUR DAYS OF NYUNGNE

On the first day offerings are made to the local gods. On the second day everyone assembles in the temple for prayers and recitations. There is a midday meal on the second day, but after that a fast is observed until the morning of the fourth and final day. An evening feast celebrates the merit that everyone has accrued.

PILGRIMAGE

Pilgrimage plays a significant part in many faiths. In the case of Islam, the pilgrimage to Mecca is central to the faith. The places associated with the Buddha hold great importance for many Buddhists, and many Christians make pilgrimages. Frequently the pilgrim is held to be subtly changed by the pilgrimage, so that the experience is seen as an intitiation into a new stage of life.

ISLAM

For the Muslim, the pilgrimage to Mecca forms one of the five basic obligations of Islam. So all Muslims hope to visit Mecca at least once in their lives. Every pilgrim (or haji) makes for the Kaaba in the courtyard of the Great Mosque. This is a cube of basalt blocks reputedly built by Abraham at God's command. At least three times during the pilgrimage the haji makes a sevenfold circuit of the Kaaba (three circuits trotting, four walking). Pilgrims may also anoint the mantle of the Kaaba with perfumes and prostrate themselves before it. Men wear the *ihram*, the traditional dress of the pilgrim. It consists of two seamless pieces of white cloth, worn so that one shoulder is bare.

HINDUISM

There are many sacred places in Hinduism. Among the most important are rivers, especially the Ganges. Another is the sacred cave at Amarnath in the Himalayas, where the god Siva and his wife Parvati are supposed to have lived. It is believed that Siva gave the secret of immortality to Parvati in the cave one night at full moon. Siva is called the destroyer, he who removes things from the world to make way for new life. Not surprisingly, many old people go on the pilgrimage to his cave, as well as numerous parents with young children. On arrival at the cave, the pilgrims make for the sacred grey pillar formed by the action of water seeping through the cave wall. Offerings of silk clothes, food, flowers and coins are left in the cave.

TIBETAN BUDDHISM

Among the holy places of Tibetan Buddhism one of the most sacred is the monastery of the Jokhang. Like other Buddhist shrines, it was closed by the Chinese regime, but when it reopened in 1979 it immediately became a goal of pilgrims once more. One image of special importance is that of Chenrezi, a spirit who is believed to have been embodied in the first of the Dalai Lamas, spritual leaders of the Tibetan Buddhists. Offerings of grain are made at the monastery and the image of a three-eyed protective deity is stuck with pins in the belief that the minds of the pilgrims will in turn be sharpened by this ritual.

CHRISTIANITY

One of the most remarkable Christian pilgrimages is the Corpus Christi pilgrimage to Qoyllur Riti in Peru. The journey involves a perilous climb up a glacier near Cuzco, to commemorate the appearance of Christ there in 1780, although a similar ritual was probably carried out in pre-Christian times. A cross is erected in the ice, prayers are said and candles lit. The mountain is said to be a home to the spirits of those who have committed mortal sins, but the pilgrims, many of whom are young men referred to as *ukukus* (or bears) are thought to be strengthened by their journey, and are thus able to withstand the evil influence. When they return the pilgrims often bring blocks of ice down the mountain with them. The ice is held to have healing powers.

Gift-giving

CHRISTMAS GIFTS
The longstanding tradition of Christmas gift-giving began with the Magi bringing gifts to the infant Christ. Their actions demonstrate several types of gift-giving: they were celebrating the birth of a child; they were acting as subjects bringing tribute to a monarch; and they were showing how giving a gift can cement a relationship.

In almost all societies people give gifts. In the West, gift-giving marks anniversaries, religious festivals and rites of passage. Elsewhere, in places as far apart as the Trobriand Islands of the southwest Pacific and the native American settlements of the northwest coasts of Canada and the United States, there are regular ceremonies that revolve around lavish gift-giving. The gifts can range widely in value, from items that can take months to make or cost a fortune to things of mainly symbolic value, like birthday cards. What do these varied gifts, and the different occasions that prompt their giving, have in common?

GIFTS FOR ALL OCCASIONS

Gift are given on all sorts of occasions in modern industrialized societies. Birthdays, naming ceremonies, weddings, anniversaries, Christmas, New Year – all of these occasions are marked by gift-giving in western societies. In addition, special rites of initiation such as one's first day at school or graduation from university are often occasions for gift-giving.

With modern social surveys it is possible to measure the amount of money spent on gifts, and the results are surprisingly high. Surveys carried out in Britain in 1968 showed that 4.3 per cent of consumer expenditure was devoted to the buying of gifts. The importance of gifts to the economy, based on these figures, was found to be forty-five times more than that of cement, a basic commodity. We can begin to see that giving has a very high economic importance.

The strength of the gift business in the West can be seen most clearly in the industry that is devoted to making and selling greetings cards for every conceivable occasion. Birthdays and Christmas or New Year are no longer enough for the card manufacturers, who actually promote what they call 'Special Days' for which cards can be bought. Mothering Sunday has been joined by Fathers' Day, and even a special day for grandmothers, to ensure that the manufacturers have a steady income throughout the year.

THE PROCESS OF EXCHANGE

What is happening when we give gifts? Most importantly, we are exchanging gifts. If a relative gives me a gift for my birthday, I know that I am usually expected to give him one on his birthday. A gift establishes or confirms a social obligation. Indeed, manufacturers promoting their products with gifts often feel that they have to offer what they describe as 'free gifts', gifts without obligation, for the deal to be attractive.

The process of exchange is so important that people often worry about the value of their gifts. Will the present be valuable enough to please the recipient, or will it be too valuable, making it difficult for the recipient to send an equivalent gift when the time comes? A recent newspaper article about the gifts presented at a British royal wedding made some interesting points about the value of gifts given by various friends and relatives of the couple. Those giving gifts ranged from members of the British royal family to friends such as prominent entertainers. The royal relatives in general gave gifts of considerably lower financial value than the famous friends. Various conclusions could be drawn from this. A possible explanation is that the relatives were more confident that a present of relatively low value would be acceptable. The friends, on the other hand tended to err on the side of extravagance, because, perhaps, they lacked confidence in the acceptability of what they had to offer.

There can be quite elaborate rules that dictate how gifts should be exchanged. In Pakistan, and among Pakistani communities in England, there is a tradition called lena-dena ('taking-giving'), which governs presents given on special occasions such as a wedding or a child's first complete reading of the Qur'an. Under this system a gift is reciprocated with one worth slightly more. This in turn creates a further debt, which is repaid with a gift worth the difference between the first two, plus a little more, and so on.

So gifts are rather like hospitality: both are expected to be reciprocated. In this, gift-giving resembles many other aspects of social life,

which are also questions of exchange. Gift-giving is a ritual embodiment of this process, which helps to bind together relationships, indeed help to unify entire societies.

Reciprocating a gift is not the only obligation involved in the exchange process. On the whole, it is forbidden to refuse a gift, for refusal signifies a snub to the giver and a denial of the obligation to give another gift in exchange. This is another similarity between gift-giving and the hospitality of the table and is seen in widely differing societies. In the industrialized West, generally one accepts gifts. The similar rules are seen in traditional societies. As an early 20th-century anthropologist studying the Andaman islands reported, 'Nobody is free to refuse the present that is offered. Everyone…tries to outdo one another in generosity.'

There are exceptions to this rule. The idea of a bribe, which can be seen as an additional gift over and above the normal payment for a service, is frowned upon in some cultures, condoned in others. The authorities have tried to eliminate bribes in many countries; but in certain cultures from Africa to Southeast Asia, bribes are accepted as a normal part of everyday and business life. Where bribes are part of the normal life of the culture, one is expected to give them, and entitled to expect something in return.

THE GIFT AND SOCIETY

There are some peoples whose entire social structure is underpinned by gift-giving. One of the most famous examples comes from the Trobriand Islands, a group of coral islands in the southwest Pacific near to Papua New Guinea. The islands were made famous in the West through the work of the anthropologist Bronislaw Malinowski, who lived for several years among the Trobriand islanders and published a book on them, *Argonauts of the Southern Pacific*, in 1922. His studies showed how central the gift was to this society.

The clearest example of this is the Trobriand ceremony called the *kula*. In the *kula*, two types of article continually circulate through the islands, passing from island to

MUTUAL BENEFIT
The gift of food to a Buddhist monk not only helps him to survive but also has an important benefit for the giver. Buddhists believe that they can accrue merit in this life or in subsequent rebirths through good deeds like giving to the monks.

island and person to person in a continuous exchange. The male islanders (only men are involved) are eager to take part in the *kula*, to which is attached great importance by the Trobriand islanders.

It is easy to see that this ceremony has a number of important and useful effects. First, many of the preparations are useful to the community, such as the building of sea-going canoes. Moreover, apart from the ritual exchanges of necklaces and bracelets, more ordinary trade is also carried on alongside the *kula*; one does not trade with one's *kula* partner, but the *kula* opens the way up for trade in general. In addition, the institution embraces and links many islands, and binds together numerous tribes. People of the area can travel from island to island confident that they will have a friendly reception.

The other well known example of gift-exchange which has been institutionalized occurs among the Kwakiutl people of northwestern North America. The ceremony is called *potlatch*, a word that means 'giving'. The most elaborate of these occurred before the end of the 19th century, although celebrated *potlatches* also took place well into the 20th century. *Potlatches* are feasts that are often designed to celebrate a number of significant events, from births and the granting of titles to peace agreements between groups. The outstanding element of each *potlatch* is the exchange of gifts, which in the 19th and early 20th centuries took place on an extraordinary scale. Blankets, oil, copper shields and trays, canoes – all would be given in vast quantities. At one ceremony in the early 20th century, approximately 33,000 blankets are said to have been exchanged.

Such an all-involving gathering must have been an effective social binding force. Such it proved even after the central authorities prohibited it: the demand for its restoration became a potent symbol of the nationalist movement among the Kwakiutl people in the first half of this century.

POTLATCH, NORTHWEST AMERICA
The Kwakiutl people of the northwestern coast of America, have a traditional ceremony called the potlatch, a

large tribal gathering involving speech-making, feasting and, above all, the large-scale giving of gifts by the host. The effect would often be to confirm or validate the social position of the host as a chief by creating a debt that most of the guests could never hope to repay. The ceremony was banned by a law of 1884, but illicit potlatches continued. The law was repealed in 1951.

ARRIVAL OF THE GUESTS

Invited guests arrive in their brightly decorated canoes at the place where the potlatch is to be held. In the background are totem poles. Seating is arranged according to a complex protocol, as are other events such as speech-making and feasting. At the climax of the ceremony, gifts are handed out. Blankets used to be the traditional gift, but nowadays a wide variety of gifts from money to clothes might be given.

GIFTS AND CURRENCY

Gifts are sometimes little different from currency, which is exchanged in return for goods or services. Sometimes a commodity is used both as a currency and as a traditional gift. The Baruya people of New Guinea use salt in this way. Salt was originally important to the Baruya because the tubers that make up much of their diet are low in sodium. The Baruya discovered that they could make salt from the ashes of the plant *Coix gigantea*, which apparently puts those who own land on which to grow these salt plants at an advantage in Baruya society. But Baruya land-owners compensate for this by making gifts of salt to relatives, in-laws and close friends. More than a third of the total of salt bars produced are redistributed in this way.

The valued salt bars are kept safely above the hearth and used mainly on special occasions such as initiations and children's naming ceremonies. The bars may also be used as currency, in exchange for a range of items from everyday tools and weapons to luxury items like ceremonial costumes.

HONOURING THE GODS AND HELPING THE POOR

Gifts have always had a role to play in religious rituals. The idea of making an offering to the gods is a long-standing one. The ancient Egyptians would give money to the priests to make offerings of food to their gods at the temples. Food would be left at the temple and, when the gods themselves did not appear to take it, the priests would return and eat the food themselves, on the gods' behalf.

The ancient Greeks had a more direct method of sending offerings. They would pour libations, liquid offerings, into a pit in the ground. There was no need of a middle-man to consume the offer on the deity's behalf.

The idea of supporting the priesthood with gifts is a longstanding one. In medieval Europe people gave one-tenth of their income (a tithe) to the church. This way of supporting the clergy is still current. In many Buddhist communities, monks are fed from alms given by the local people. Elsewhere religion encourages the rich to give to the poor. This is as likely to be in the interests of the giver as of the recipient. It is one of the fundamental duties of Islam, for example, to pay a special tax for charitable purposes. Christians, too, are encouraged to give to the poor. Christ, in the Sermon on the Mount, said that alms should be given discreetly: the Christian's reward would come from God and not from any person who saw the gift being made. The Arab word *sadaka* and the Hebrew *zedaqa* originally meant 'justice', but now mean 'alms'.

A similar emphasis on alms-giving can be found in other societies. Among the Hausa people of West Africa, for example, fever may spread when the corn is ripe. A way of alleviating the fever and thus protecting

STONE COINS
The Pacific Yap people, use stone discs in payment of debts and in settlement of disputes.

THE KULA

The people of the Trobriand Islands are bound by a traditional form of exchange called the kula. *Two types of item are exchanged in the* kula. *Long necklaces of red shell move clockwise around the group of islands; bracelets of white shell travel counterclockwise. Each participant in the* kula *holds an item for a short time before handing it on.*

THE BENEFITS OF EXCHANGE

The ritual of the *kula* gives the Trobriand islanders a way of meeting people from other islands and is a means by which the different tribes in the islands remain politically united. The building of sea-going canoes and the encouragement of ordinary trade are examples of other spin-off benefits of the *kula*.

THE RITUALS OF EXCHANGE

A sea-going canoe sets sail from one island to the next. On board are the male participants in the *kula*, together with the necklaces or bracelets which they are going to exchange. On arrival at the next island, the men ceremonially offer a necklace to the chief. The much-travelled necklace will have a long ritual history, and the people who are exchanging it may relate its pedigree, telling who has held it and on which islands. Clay pots that are part of a more conventional trade that takes place at the same time as the ritual exchange may also be loaded onto a canoe.

everyone, is to give grain to the poor. Gifts to the poor may also be held to please the spirits of the dead.

BRINGING TRIBUTE

Another form of gift with a long history is tribute. This is the goods brought to a ruler by subject peoples, as an indication of loyalty and submission.

There are numerous ancient examples of tribute, from Nubians bringing gold to the ancient Egyptian pharaohs to the subject people of the Persian empire queueing up to bring tribute to the emperor at the great ceremonial palace at Persepolis. Their images can still be seen, carved in relief beside the staircases to the great audience chamber at Persepolis, the Bactrians bringing their camels, the Medes their horses, Ethiopians with elephant tusks, others with rich cloth or valuable jewellery.

Such traditions still continue in some areas. Ethiopian peasants are traditionally expected to pay tribute in return for their right to hold land. And in other parts of Africa, tribute is given to local chiefs in return for hospitality (public feasts) and protection at times of unrest. Such systems are not far in their role and effects from the formal taxation imposed by western governments in return for services. This is another way in which present-giving and monetary exchange are similar.

Local leaders (often referred to as 'big men') in the Melanesian Islands use tribute systems to reinforce their power. The Melanesian big man achieves his status as chief by attracting a group of loyal followers. To do this he must somehow amass an impressive fortune (generally made up of pigs, foodstuffs and shell money), which he can distribute among his followers in a way that brings him a reputation for great generosity. He holds public giveaways to demonstrate this generosity, thereby increasing the number of people who are indebted to him and who thus form part of his following.

Similar to the tribute system is the tradition that ambassadors bring gifts when they visit a foreign ruler or an opposite number from another state. But whereas the tribute system tends to emphasize the power of the recipient over the giver, an ambassadorial gift is more likely to be intended to cement a relationship of equals.

THE SPIRIT OF THE GIFT

But gift-giving is more than simple economic exchange. Gifts cement personal relationships and provide a means of communications between loved ones. People say that a gift lets the recipient know we are thinking of them, that we want to make the person 'feel special'. We want to make people feel wanted, to feel part of our social or family group. We give presents to make amends, to say 'I'm sorry'. Sometimes we try hard to find a present that someone will like or enjoy; sometimes we give things that we would feel comfortable with. In all these cases, the gifts are sending out messages – often very eloquent ones.

Gifts frequently have a spiritual dimension. Hindu tradition, for example, sees a gift as a kind of sacrifice. This does not mean simply that the giver has made an economic sacrifice in order to give a present. It also means that the gift is a kind of surrogate for, or symbol of, the donor. With such a strong link between the gift and the giver, it is not surprising that the rules of exchange seen in so many places do not operate in these circumstances. One is not expected to give a similar gift in exchange. Indeed, one is not even under obligation to accept the gift in the first place.

People in the West often talk about presents in a similar, rather mystical, way. A woman whose mother had died some years ago described the many gifts around her house that her mother had given her over the years: 'I

FREE FEAST
In the Solomon Islands, a traditional way of giving was to organize a free feast. The host, who would be someone aspiring to the status of leader or 'big man', would amass hundreds of pigs and large amounts of shell money. These would be given to the host's social rival, with the aim of shaming him into the admission that he could not reciprocate with gifts of equivalent value. A special wooden openwork tower was constructed, in which the food for the feast was displayed so that all could see and marvel at the generosity of the host.

THE TRIUMPH OF HOSPITALITY
A series of feasts might go on for years, until one of the parties was finally defeated through his inability to match his rival's bounty. Finally, the winner's high social status would be acknowledged. In the language of the islanders, 'leader' and 'giver of feasts' are synonymous.

appreciate these, and they mean something to me because I remember the occasion they were given on, and that it was from my mother, and the relationship we've had.' The gifts remain, and keep the memory of the relationship alive. This woman felt the same about the gifts she gave to others. She hoped that the recipients would look at the things in years to come and remember her.

Emotions like these reveal the positive spirit that still lies behind gift-giving. They give the lie to the notion put forward by the anthropologist Claude Lévi-Strauss that modern western gift-giving was highly wasteful, with much duplication of presents, like a modern caricature of the Kwakiutl *potlatch*. Studies in Canada and elsewhere have shown that this is not the case. Gifts are not, on the whole, duplicated, even at Christmas time when so many presents are given. And the emotional benefit for the participants in the gift-exchange is reason alone for it to continue.

Dispute-settlement

When there is a dispute between two or more people, it is not always possible to resolve it by rational argument. So societies everywhere have evolved ways to settle disputes, to decide who is right and who is wrong in a way that will be accepted by both parties, and to allocate punishment or compensation if these are deemed necessary.

Exactly how disputes are settled varies greatly from place to place, and the methods used say much about the values of each society. In some places, the dispute is settled by trials of a particular quality that will set the victor apart from his or her opponent. It might be the person's physical strength, their ability to sing, or their ability to bring convincing evidence. Sometimes the social pressures to solve the dispute can be so strong that the participants are forced to sort it out for themselves in a way that will benefit the rest of the society. In other places, the arbitration of a key person, a leader or a judge, is sought and is accepted by both parties as binding. Usually, that person's power to pass sentence or apportion blame will be based on experience. A western lawyer will be appointed as a judge only after years of practising law. The rulings of a Melanesian 'big man', who has legal power because of his social position, will be heeded only if he can demonstrate that his judgements are sound.

The ability of the judge to impose sanctions that will bring about correct behaviour is an important aspect of his or her power. Most societies expect wrongdoers to be punished in some way and do not accept that the dispute is settled if no appropriate punishment is meted out. Imprisonment, fine, restriction of movement or of access to an aggrieved party, corporal or capital punishment, are all used as punishments in different cultures and in different circumstances. But the feeling that the punishment should match the severity and type of offence is common in most places.

The concept of 'the law' is something that varies widely. Clearly, different states have different laws. But the differences go deeper than this. Many societies do not use a codified system of laws like those favoured in the West. In such societies the concept of legality is much more fluid than is often the case where there is a written legal system.

FEUDING

One of the most simple patterns of behaviour that results from a dispute is the feud. An aggrieved party or their kin seek vengeance for a wrong; the vengeance is wrought but itself provokes counter-vengeance, and so on. Disputes like this between families or tribes have gone on for generations.

Psychologists tell us that the desire for revenge is a very basic human emotion. And there have certainly been feuds throughout history. In Homer's ancient Greek epic *The Iliad*, the Greeks go to war against the Trojans because the Trojan Paris has eloped with Helen, wife of the Greek King Menelaus.

Feuds are still common in the modern world. The 20th century has seen a strong tradition of feuding in countries as diverse as Italy and Ecuador. The Jibaro Indians of Ecuador, for example, are a warrior people with a strong tradition of independence, living not in villages but as separate families or small groups of families in fortified wooden houses built often on the tops of hills. Such isolation tends to reduce the likelihood of inter-family disputes, but these nevertheless still occur. Adultery and the abduction of women by men from another social group are frequent causes of feuding between groups.

RESOLVING CONFLICTS
Through history, disputes
have been settled by the
real or ritualized conflicts
of war, the joust or boxing
ring, or by the judgement
of the courts or the chief.

Among the Jibaro, if a murder is committed, a life is taken in return. There is a religious imperative for this, since they consider that the soul of the dead person requires the survivors to take revenge. If the original murderer admits guilt, then this is the end of the matter: justice has been done. But if the first killer will not admit his guilt, a feud is likely to develop since any life that is then taken in revenge will be held to have been taken unjustly.

RITUAL CONTESTS

A feud is not a way of settling a dispute; rather, it tends to perpetuate the conflict. So many societies have found ways to avoid the endless

TRIAL BY ORDEAL

The notion of trial by ordeal is rather like trial by combat. The parties in a dispute accept a challenge. They agree to undergo an ordeal, such as walking across a fire or plunging a hand into boiling water. The victor is the one who comes out of the ordeal least scathed. Usually it is held that gods or spirits will help the innocent party and ensure that the guilty will be injured. To refuse to accept the challenge is also usually thought to imply guilt.

THE PHILIPPINES

The Ifugao people of the Philippines use ordeals to reach judgements in criminal cases and property disputes. A popular method is the hot-water ordeal, in which each of the parties must put a hand into a pot of boiling water, pull out a pebble, and then replace the pebble. The person who is innocent or in the right will be less badly burned than someone who is guilty or in the wrong.

THE SOLOMON ISLANDS

The Kwaio of the Solomon Islands also use ordeals, emphasizing the role of ancestor-spirits in the proceedings. Even a guilty person may pray to an ancestor for help. Putting in a wrongful plea of not guilty, surviving the ordeal unscathed, and being let off is frequently attributed to the intervention of a well-disposed ancestor spirit, as seen here.

violence of the feud without dispensing with the need for retaliation. In medieval Europe, for example, there was a strong tradition of 'trial by combat', in which the two opposing parties or their champions would fight according to strict rules. God, the medieval Christians argued, would favour the innocent or aggrieved party, who would therefore prevail.

Among the Inuits of Alaska, Baffinland and Siberia, wrestling is traditionally used to resolve disputes. The tribes living along the Arctic Circle from Hudson Bay to the Bering Straits favour a type of struggle called buffeting. The opponents face each other and hit one another with straight-armed blows to

the side of the head. Eventually one of the duellers is knocked out and the other is declared the winner. The winner's social esteem is enhanced; the loser has to submit to a downgrading of social rank.

The Greenland Inuits add head-butting to the duellers' repertoire. But the Greenlanders do not limit themselves to physical combat. Their favourite method of dispute-settlement is the song duel. Such contests involve the use of both traditional and specially composed songs that heap insults on the opponent. The duel itself may last, on and off, for months or even years, although most are over much sooner. Sometimes the insults are explicit, as in this example sung to a man who has stolen his opponent's wife:

> *An impudent, black-skinned oaf has stolen her,*
> *Has tried to belittle her.*
> *A miserable wretch who loves human flesh—*
> *A cannibal from famine days.*

When the opponents have finished singing, the spectators pass judgement in favour of one of them. There is no attempt to mete out punishment, but there is a feeling of relief that the conflict has been played out. The two parties can resume their lives, and they often remain the best of friends when the duel is over. The duel has defused the dispute. It has also provided great entertainment for the rest of the community.

CONTEST AND JUDGEMENT

One society in which the combination of an artistic performance and a formal hearing has been seen clearly is the Tiv of northern Nigeria. A man with a grievance waits until nightfall when everything is quiet. Then he begins a loud song, accompanied by drumming, that describes how the person has

SINGING CONTEST
The singing contest is a traditional way of resolving disputes among Inuit peoples.

been ill-treated and pours scorn on the opponent. The song may well be taken up by the relatives of the singer, making a loud chorus and ensuring that the details of the case can be heard far out into the night.

The opponent responds with a song of his own, putting the case from his point of view. This may go on for several nights, with each rival singing in his own compound and the rival strains echoing across the night. When the inspiration of the protagonists runs out, professional singers may be hired to carry on the duel, and beer may be served in each of the compounds as an encouragement for others to join in the song and dance.

In former times, the rival singing and

EXPRESSING GRIEVANCES
From Nigeria to New Guinea, grievances are
aired in songs to the accompaniment of a drum.

dancing would often turn into brawling.
A fight between the two opponents would
develop, and whoever won the fight would be
the victor in the dispute. Nowadays, the
dispute is likely to be resolved differently.
When the singing reaches a climax, or looks as
if it will develop into a brawl, the local leader
calls the opponents to his compound and
listens to them both singing and drumming.
Both participants in the dispute are then given
the chance to present their case and the leader
makes a formal decision. The songs can have
some influence on the judgement, but it is

perfectly possible for the person with the best
songs to lose the case – the facts of the matter
are taken into full consideration.

In some places, music is used purely to
express anger or a grievance, not as part of a
competition but as a prelude to some sort of
hearing. The Tangu people of the north coast
of New Guinea use rapid drumming on a slit-
gong to do this. Such drumming may bring the
local men together to eat and hear the speeches
of the parties in a gathering called
br'ngun'guni. Eating is an important part of
the dispute settlement, since crimes are often to
do with the theft of food or resources, and the
formal offering of food helps to re-establish
the equilibrium. The aim is not so much to
make a legal judgement on one or other of the
opponents, but to allow the personal
relationships openly to work themselves out.

Thus the Tangu have what is in some ways
an informal method of resolving disputes.
Many societies have both formal and informal
methods. This is especially common in Africa,
where there may be highly formal courts
together with less formal semi-legal meetings
that are also there to resolve differences
between individuals. One example is the
'moot' of the Kpelle people of central Liberia.

The Kpelle have recourse to the various
constitutional courts available in Liberia, the
highest of which is that of a paramount chief.
As in many societies, there are different levels
of court to try different kinds of cases. These
courts are successful in resolving many types
of dispute, but have a limited success with
matrimonial cases: men and women often
prefer to take their domestic disputes to some
less formal meeting, such as a moot.

The meeting is called by the person with
the grievance, who chooses a kinsman who is
also a town chief or elder to act as mediator. It
is held in the complainant's home and people
are frequently squashed into all the available
space: the audience often overflows out onto
the verandah.

VARIETIES OF JUSTICE
Since before the judgment of Solomon, most cultures have preferred the authority of a specially appointed judge to the rough justice of the outlaw or avenger.

After a blessing pronounced by the elder, the hearing begins with a speech by the complainant, who is then questioned searchingly by all present. The accused then speaks and is similarly questioned. Witnesses may also speak and answer questions. Then the mediator and anyone present who wants to voice an opinion make their observations on the case before the mediator sums up on the basis of the general consensus. The person who is held to be to blame then formally apologises to the wronged party, presenting small gifts (of rice, some coins, or clothing) to them. The victor is also expected to give a token gift (usually a small coin) to the guilty person. The latter must also pay 'costs', in the form of rum or beer to the mediator and the others who have heard the case.

The moot offers a quick form of justice and it provides a decision that has the backing of the majority of those present. The giving and returning of token gifts helps to heal the breach and to confirm that the grievances have been settled. The moot does not have the power to impose heavy punishments such as large fines or jail sentences, but it is very good at resolving minor disputes.

MODERN JUSTICE

The courts and procedures that modern industrialized societies use to resolve their disputes are just as ritualized as, and in some cases a good deal more archaic than, their traditional counterparts. The special costumes worn by judges and lawyers, the gowns, the specialized legal language and the titles by which members of the court are referred ('your honour', 'm'lud') create an atmosphere steeped in ritual. Court architecture, which separates the judge or magistrate, the counsel, witnesses, accused and lookers-on, adds further elements of ritual.

Such conventions have many different effects. They are held to inspire respect for the law and its decisions. They depersonalize the lawyers, so that it is less possible to be resentful of those who try a case or pass a sentence. In addition, they formalize the proceedings, so that it is clear that they are being carried out correctly.

In some places the social power of the law is so great that people resort to the law at the least provocation. Social commentators often talk about modern American society in this way. There are other examples. Among the Subanun peoples of the Philippines are groups that regard litigation amost as a sort of social game. As one anthropologist put it 'A festivity without litigation is almost as unthinkable as one without drink.' Law cases are contests of skill in which one takes part in order to win and play again. And amongst the African Barotse people it is said that people will actually commit a crime in order to go to court. The social power of the law can work in unexpected ways.

WITCHCRAFT AND POSSESSION

Special machinery often has to be set up to settle disputes where the supernatural is allegedly at the root of the problem. This can be the case with witchcraft and sorcery, in

WITCHCRAFT
The Zande of southern Sudan determine the truth by assessing the effect of poison on a chicken.

which one person is said to have used supernatural powers to influence or harm another. The Zande of southern Sudan are a people with a strong tradition of witchcraft and sorcery. In the past, disputes often arose because it was alleged that one person had practised sorcery on another.

The Zande would blame witchcraft for all sorts of abnormal happenings. For example, someone attacked by an animal when out hunting is not simply the victim of a random accident. He may have been singled out by an enemy who has performed witchcraft on him. In such a situation, it was the responsibility of the chief to find out whether witchcraft has been used and if so, by whom. He was also called upon to work magic to provide revenge for any wrongdoing.

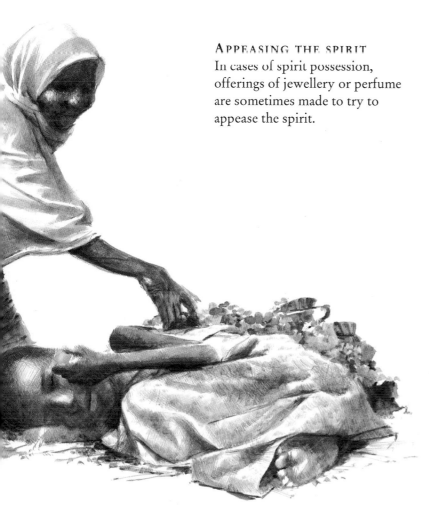

APPEASING THE SPIRIT
In cases of spirit possession, offerings of jewellery or perfume are sometimes made to try to appease the spirit.

Various techniques were used to find out what had happened. The chief might simply question the complainant. He kept abreast of local news and gossip and this knowledge informed his questions. But a more ritualistic method of divination could also be employed. The aggrieved party would administer an alkaloidal poison called *benge* to a chicken. He would then announce his suspicions and declaim the phrase 'Oracle, if such is the case, kill the chicken'. Further tests with other chickens could be used to confirm the judgement. These divinations were so important to the Zande that many households kept a fowl-house with an ample supply of the birds, specifically for this purpose.

The aggrieved person would then take his findings to the chief's court, where the chief would test the claim with his own chicken oracle. If the results were positive, the person responsible for the sorcery would be sent for and ordered to put a stop to the evil influence.

Sometimes the dispute can be between the human and spirit world as when, for example, a person is held to be possessed by a spirit. The Muslim Somali people explain many ills in this way. The problem is resolved by appeasing the spirit by lavish gifts.

SOCIAL PRESSURES

Most societies put informal pressures on members to resolve conflicts. We have already looked in passing at the way in which eating together brings disputing people closer in some societies, notably in New Guinea. Here, as in many societies, hospitality is an important virtue, and if you share food with someone, you are their friend. When there is a dispute, this can work both ways. A sudden refusal to eat with a neighbour makes the conflict obvious. But in situations where food is scarce and where people live in close communities, where the food eaten by different families may be grown in the same plot or cooked over the same fire, the refusal to eat together can soon seem pointless. We have to survive, both physically and socially. And so a return to the common table can lead to an end of a quarrel, a beginning of peace.

A similar technique for settling differences is also used in the developed world. The point will often come in a dispute when both sides tacitly recognize that there is little point in continuing. At this point, an invitation to 'bury the hatchet' over a drink may bring about an effective conclusion to the conflict.

A story recorded by the contemporary anthropologist Elizabeth Colson when she was working in Tonga illustrates another way in which informal social pressures can work. A dispute broke out between the Eland and Lion clans when an Eland man killed a Lion man from a neighbouring village. The police arrested the guilty man, who was tried and sentenced to a year in prison. The Lion clan were not satisfied with this sentence and severed relations with the Eland people living nearby. But because there was intermarriage between the two clans, this caused difficulties for some people. Eland wives with Lion husbands were taunted by their kinsfolk for consorting with the enemy. Gradually, as the feud got worse, these wives and their in-laws began to put pressure on their menfolk to settle the dispute.

The Elands offered compensation to the Lions, this was accepted, and peace returned. But the Elands were slow in paying the compensation. A boy of mixed Eland-Lion parentage died and the death was blamed on the wrath of the unavenged spirit of the dead Lion man. Once more, pressure was put on the Elands to pay, which they did, bringing peace.

LARGE-SCALE DISPUTES
War – dispute on a large scale, involving many people and much bloodshed – has developed its own sets of procedures to bring about

peace. Sometimes the machinery of conflict resolution is very similar to that for individual disputes. A war between the followers of local leaders in a chiefdom like Polynesia might be resolved by appealing to the chief himself. On a larger scale, the Security Council of the United Nations has been vested with primary responsibility for the maintenance of international peace and security.

There are special customs when it comes to making peace between tribes or nations. These rituals often reflect the gravity of the situation, the feeling that the solution to a conflict of such importance needs some high form of sanction if it is to hold. Sometimes it is a question of calling on the supernatural. In Borneo, for example, it was the custom for each of the parties to swear an oath of peace. As they did this, each would kill a pig, the idea being that the animal's spirit would tell the gods that the oath had been sworn.

The negotiations that lead to peace between modern warring nations have their own rituals. Before anyone sits down at a table to discuss the terms of the peace, there are likely to be 'negotiations about the negotiations', in which are discussed matters such as the choice of the negotiators and chair, the venue for the meeting, and the overall framework of the discussion. Such preliminary talks are designed to provide a forum that is acceptable and recognised by all parties as fair. And when they do begin, the rituals of international diplomacy – the secrecy, the issuing of discreetly 'coded' messages (in which a virtual fist fight can be repesented as a 'frank exchange', for example), the show of courtesy to one's opponents, and so on – help to smooth the way and allow all sides to save face.

As with individual disputes, public pressure, often highly ritualized, can also be brought to bear. The demonstration, is a highly visible way in which large numbers of people can make their feelings known. But demonstrations are not merely symbolic:

demonstrators hope to bring about real change and sometimes they do. Nevertheless, the demonstration is a way of ritualizing protest.

The settlement of both personal and international disputes, then, involves a range of rituals. Bringing together two antagonistic parties, whether they are individuals in a tribal society with a domestic grievance or world leaders meeting at the United Nations, frequently calls for the most ingenious rituals that humanity has been able to devise. What social equilibrium we have owes much to this ingenuity.

MARCHING ON

The public demonstration has become one of the most well known ways of registering protest. Most demonstrations include a march of which the destination has some key role in the dispute or it may simply be a conveniently situated open space that is large enough for a public meeting. Sometimes the place may have a special significance – the site of a battle or the statue of a leader. Protesters usually carry banners or placards. A demonstration may not actually settle a dispute, but it can be a potent way to bring a conflict to a head.

A TRADITION OF PROTEST
We may think of demonstrations as a modern phenomenon, but they have taken place for centuries. In this illustration, marchers during an early 20th-century revolution are joined by their spiritual successors – contemporary anti-nuclear protestors.

SPIRITUALITY

RELIGION AND ART:
TRANSCENDING THE EVERYDAY WORLD

Humans have always strived for experiences beyond the everyday. Perhaps the two strongest and longest-lasting products of this search have been religion and art. Some of the earliest and most fascinating artefacts left behind by our ancestors are sculptures, and these works of art may well portray goddesses and gods, indicating that curiosity about the metaphysical dates from the very beginnings of human history.

Religions of all kinds have attempted to provide answers to the great questions posed by humankind since the earliest times about the purpose of life and whether there is an all-powerful force governing or guiding our actions. The arts have provided expression for some of these concerns, by examining, for example, the nature of beauty, harmony and suffering. Not surprisingly, the worlds of art and religion touch at many points.

PEOPLE OF POWER

Religious leaders have always had a certain power. Whether presiding over a rain-making festival or a midsummer celebration, the priests of former times must have seemed to wield an awesome influence. Interestingly enough, people often feel the same way about artists. In some Pacific communities, it is held to be dangerous to touch an artist's hands after he has been working. In many places, the artist is looked upon as a sort of seer, someone with special insights and whose opinion is often sought.

RITUALS OF THE SPIRIT

Both art and religion are surrounded by ritual. The worship and prayer of the organized religions take place in set ways, at particular times. There are processions, singing, as well as dancing in some cultures – all the familiar elements of ritual. Even the more contemplative religions, such as Zen Buddhism, have their set procedures, which, through constant repetition by the individual, take on the role of rituals. And music and dance can have special roles in inducing religious trances and 'heightened' states of mind.

Artists, too, have their rituals, ranging from the elaborate etiquette of a Melanesian mask house to the private superstitions of the western actor. In both cases, it is often held that the art – the mask or the theatrical performance – will be bereft of its power if the rituals are ignored.

Like the other rituals described in this book, the rituals of religion and art play vital social roles. They may either support forces of personal and social stability or they may foster new ways of thinking and social change. But most of all they lead both participants and spectators beyond the everyday, to flights of the imagination and visions of the infinite.

Worship

Religion flourishes in nearly all human societies. It dominates many of the customs and rituals that have been described in this book. In many societies the rites of passage, for example, are presided over by the representatives of the local religion, the priests. Even in the West, where there is less religious observance than anywhere, many still go to church, temple, or synagogue to take part in the ceremonies that punctuate our lives.

REASONS FOR RELIGION

One of the most important functions of any religion is to help to explain the unknown. What was the origin of the world? What happens when we die? What is the purpose of life? What is in the distant heavens? Is there a need for suffering? Questions like these have required a special kind of answer, one that draws on some idea of a world outside our own, a world of spirits, perhaps, or of gods and goddesses. Such a world needs interpretation, and priests have traditionally filled the role of interpreters and mediators between the supernatural and natural worlds.

But religion is not there simply to provide answers. It often provides the theoretical basis and moral weight for codes of behaviour that are essential to the good ordering of society. Religion is also a response to a widespread human need to look beyond the basic requirements of material survival, to feed the spirit in addition to the body and the mind. Such a turning to 'higher things' almost invariably demands special procedures designed to promote obedience or devotion to the deity, respect for the priest, and to encourage the adoption of a frame of mind on the part of the worshipper that is conducive to

THE VARIETIES OF RELIGION
The religions of the world take many forms, from the various types of animism, with their numerous nature spirits, to the monotheistic religions, like Islam and Christianity. In Buddhism, by contrast, the individual's path to enlightenment is more important than the worship of any deity.

spirituality. Religious observance, in other words, demands rituals.

In most religions priests are mediators, and the ceremonies over which they preside set up links between the human and supernatural worlds. In addition, the priest stands guard over the tradition of which he is a part. He is responsible for ensuring correct observance of the laws and ideas central to the religion he represents.

TRADITIONAL RELIGIONS

Religions dependent on an oral tradition probably began very early in the history of humankind in response to human needs to know and explain. All around the world, particularly in Africa, North and South America, Australia and Oceania a variety of such oral traditions survive.

Many are animist religions, which see the

BAG PEOPLE, NEW GUINEA
This mask is used in rituals to celebrate the earth goddess Nimba.

RELIGIONS OF NATURE
Many traditional religions are founded in nature and the elements. The environment is ascribed sacred qualities and rituals are used to try to control it, for example, to ensure good weather for crops. These illustrations are just a few examples of the worship of the many different nature spirits all over the world.

presence of special powers in nature. Everything in the natural world has a soul and there are good and bad nature spirits everywhere. In many traditional societies, certain creatures are believed to have special powers – monkeys in Zaire, fish in the south seas, beavers in North America.

Another familiar set of traditional beliefs surrounds the notion of the afterlife. Ancestor spirits are important to many peoples. In

KWAKIUTL PEOPLE, NORTH AMERICA
Rattle representing the thunder god.

SOLOMON ISLANDS
Canoe figurehead carved in the form of a bird spirit.

AZTEC PEOPLE, MEXICO
Incense burner in the form of the fire god Huehueteotl.

Africa, ancestor spirits are worshipped through objects that symbolize or embody the ancestor. For the Bambara people of Mali, this is the central pillar of the hut; for other peoples the ancestor is represented by an old empty seat. For the Kwakiutl of northwest America, the totem pole symbolizes the ancestors.

In addition to animal, plant and ancestor spirits, some traditional religions also recognize spirits of the sky, the waters, the earth, the rain, and other elemental forces. Many Arctic peoples, for example, have gods of the thunder, the sun, or the sea. In some traditional societies, one god is supreme and has ultimate power over the other deities and over people.

Traditional gods have their roots in the often harsh environments of the people who worship them. The need to placate these gods to ensure survival governs many of the hunting and agricultural customs described elsewhere in this book.

In an environment where spirits, both benevolent and threatening, are held to abound, a person can be harmed or threatened by a spirit at any time. In traditional societies, when this happens, a shaman (priest or medicine man) is summoned. He or she fulfils the modern roles of priest, doctor, and psychiatrist. A ceremony may take place in which the shaman's own spirit is freed to search out the malevolent spirit and direct it away from its victim.

Other rituals are to allow communication with the spirit world. Thanks may be given for good fortune or a good harvest, or the people may wish to calm what they believe to be angry or troubled spirits or gods. In either case there may be a sacrifice, usually of an animal that has some sort of value to the community. In Africa, for example, an animal such as a sheep, hen or bull may be sacrificed. The Ainu people of Japan would sacrifice a bear.

Alternatively, the spirits might be contacted through prayers, a method favoured by people

FIRE, LIGHT AND RITUAL

Many religions use the symbolism of light in their rituals. Light in the form of fire is used in traditional religions as a focus for dancing or as a basis for meditation. It may also be a force with which initiates have to come to terms by fire-walking. In many religions fire is tamed in the form of candles that are lit in the home as well as in the church or temple.

HINDU
In the ceremony of Arti, the priest carries five candles.

JEWISH
The lighting of candles marks the Shabat (sabbath).

FIJI
Firewalkers dash through hot coals with a minimum of pain.

PUEBLO INDIAN
Fireside meditation on the god of thunder.

as widely separated as Inuit hunters and Amazonian Indians. Elaborate festivals may be held in order to appease or please the spirits and thereby ensure the food supply or favourable weather.

From Africa to the Amazon, and Siberia to the South Seas, those presiding over spirit ceremonies often wear masks. Sometimes the mask can help the shaman to imitate or impersonate a spirit. Sometimes it carries the image of a spirit, like the tall masks used in Burkina Faso in West Africa, on which humanoid deities are portrayed above heads of antelopes. Masks, with their stylized and often beautiful designs, are often worn with a costume that disguises the wearer. Together with dance and music, a mask helps people to believe that the spirit is present behind it. Such ceremonies are one of the most powerful means by which the shaman brings the spirit world close to the people.

In some cultures, drugs are also used to help make a connection with the spirit world. These can produce a trance-like state or weird and fantastic visions, either of which may seem to observers and participants like evidence of contact with another kind of reality.

Whether it is through hallucinogens, masks, song, dance, or a combination of these, that the shaman communicates with the spirit world, the methods set the mediator apart from the rest of the society. Only members of a select group know how to make the masks correctly, and perform the music and dances; only the initiates know where to gather the sacred herbs or hallucinogenic mushrooms, and how much of the substances to use to create the desired effect. And so the mysterious process of communication with the spirits is given yet more mystery, confirming once again the power of the priestly class.

This element of mystery is also retained in certain branches of modern organized religion. For example, Tantric Buddhists, Islamic Sufis, and the Jewish students of the Kabbalah all

POSITIONS FOR PRAYER

People of different religions communicate with their gods in many different ways. The prayer may be expressed as a ringing chant, a loud appeal, a low mumble, or the person praying may be completely silent. But whatever the medium, the intensity of the message is reinforced by the rituals of prayer. The use of incense, or focusing on candles, or icons can help to concentrate the mind and exclude other thoughts. The adoption of a particular bodily position reinforces the special nature of the occasion. Putting the hands together, seen in several religions, may originally have been encouraged to stop extraneous movements. Closing the eyes during prayer may help to shut out distractions. Kneeling or prostrating oneself indicates submission to a powerful deity.

KNEELING
A Muslim kneels, head down, on a prayer mat, placed to face the holy city of Mecca.

HANDS CLASPED
Christians of all denominations traditionally pray with the hands clasped together.

PRAYER BEADS
People of many religions use beads to help count the number of times a prayer has been said.

LOTUS POSITION
Buddhists may meditate in the yogic lotus position.

emphasize the mysterious qualities of their particular religions.

THE IMPORTANCE OF THE PRIEST

In early societies the power of the priest was clear. With their ability to mediate between the gods and the people, priests had effective control over vital aspects of everyday life such as crop yields. A good planting or harvesting ceremony would ensure a rich crop the next season, and the continued survival of the people. Priests were seen to hold the power of life or death with ceremonies of healing that, properly conducted, could enable individuals to recover from illness. (See also Hunting and Harvesting, pages 116-127, and Healing, pages 140-9.) Given such power, respect for the priesthood is logical, as is supporting priests with gifts of alms and a share of the harvest, and allowing them to build up their own hierarchies and power structures.

The importance of the priest is emphasized in many religions by the way in which he or she is dressed. In many of the Christian churches, for example, priests wear flowing robes – rich red and gold in the Orthodox church, for example, white in many Anglican churches, and a rainbow of colours from scarlet to black in the Catholic church. The spiritual leaders of Islam and those of Buddhism also wear garments that help distinguish them from the rest of society. Priestly garb is not always elaborate. Monks and nuns, both Buddhist and Christian, wear clothes that mark them out as separate, while also, by their simplicity, suggesting a life of sacrifice and denial. Some religions have rejected priestly garments. In many Protestant nonconformist churches, the person leading the service wears ordinary clothes and indeed may not be a priest at all. Jewish Rabbis are not marked out by particular clothes, although every adult Jewish male wears a special garment for prayers at the synagogue.

ANGLICAN PRIEST, ENGLAND

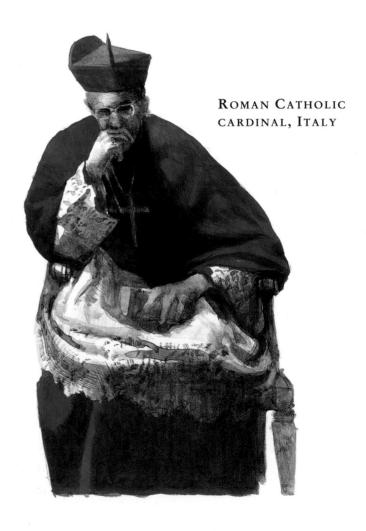

ROMAN CATHOLIC CARDINAL, ITALY

PENTECOSTAL PRIEST,
SOUTH PACIFIC

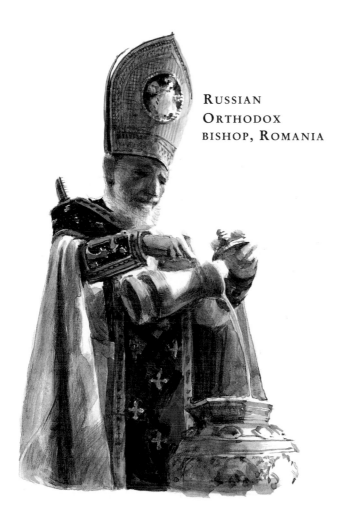

RUSSIAN
ORTHODOX
BISHOP, ROMANIA

SACRED PLACES

Religious rituals are usually held in special places that have been built or set aside for the purpose. Before the first man-made churches and temples, people looked to nature for their sacred places. Mountains were often favoured. In many cultures the gods are thought to dwell in the apparently infinite spaces of the sky; to climb a mountain is to get a little closer to the gods. The ancient Greek gods even lived on a mountain, Mount Olympus.

The world's watery places can also have sacred associations. The power of the sea – its storms, its waves, its tides – inspired many peoples to conceive of sea gods, to whom sacrifices were made. Rivers, too, are frequently held to be sacred. They have been used in purification ceremonies and initiations for thousands of years. Even today, the Ganges, and, to a lesser extent, all rivers, are sacred in Hinduism.

Caves provided secret places, where some of our earliest ancestors probably gathered to carry out religious ceremonies. Most authorities believe that the caves in which much of the earliest art has been found were probably religious sites. No one knows what sort of rites took place there – perhaps the ceremonies were to do with hunting, perhaps with fertility. But their seclusion and their decoration made them places apart indeed.

Later peoples constructed buildings specifically for conducting their religious rites. Such temples gave the rites more privacy, and marked as something special any rite that took place within. The temple could exclude outsiders, a factor that became more important as priests began to wield their power more widely. It was no accident that many of the temples of early civilizations were made to resemble mountains. The great ziggurats of the Mesopotamian civilizations of the Middle East and the pyramidal temples of the central American civilizations were like platforms, to raise the priests nearer to the gods and remove them from the mundane level of the rest of society. Buddhists created temple-mountains, too. But these, rather than being designed to exclude outsiders, were meant to symbolize the path that the Buddhist climbs towards enlightenment. As Christianity developed, church design also drew on the image of the temple mountain, with church spires pointing towards the heavens.

In some cultures the idea of the cave temple was developed. Thus the Egyptian pharaohs had a temple cut out of the cliff-face at Abu Simbel and, in parts of India, elaborate Hindu, Buddhist and Jain temples were cut into the solid rock.

HOLY PLACES ENDURE

Endurance seems to be a particular feature of the world's holy places. Once a place has been sanctified by one religion, it will remain holy, even when that religion has been replaced by a different faith. Sometimes this holy quality is commemorated by special rituals. Perhaps the world's most prominent example of a place of enduring sanctity is the city of Jerusalem, which includes sites that are sacred to Jews, Christians and Muslims.

WAILING WALL
Jews come to the Western Wall to mourn the destruction of the Temple and the exile of their people.

HOLY SEPULCHRE
The church of the Holy Sepulchre, the site of Christ's tomb, is a focus of Christian pilgrimage. It is shared by the Orthodox, Roman Catholic, Armenian, Syrian and Coptic churches.

DOME OF THE ROCK
The Dome of the Rock, traditionally the site where Abraham prepared to sacrifice his son Isaac, is a place of pilgrimage for Muslims and one of the wonders of the Islamic world.

Many sites of religious worship, in use for thousands of years, seem to the faithful to have a special quality of holiness about them. Such places may be associated with important events in the history of the religion and thus they may become places of pilgrimage too. But whether or not this is the case, part of the intensity of the experience during a religious ceremony often comes about because it takes place in specially created surroundings.

ENTERING THE SPECIAL PLACE

Most religions have evolved set procedures for entering their places of worship, and for preparing oneself for the ritual that will take

place inside. In Islam, for example, the faithful must wash and remove their shoes before entering the mosque. There are, therefore, washing facilities near the entrance. Even non-Muslim visitors are required to remove their shoes. Hindus also remove their shoes – before entering the main part of the temple. Catholic Christians make the sign of the cross with holy water from a container called a stoup near the door of the church. Other Christians may cross themselves as they enter, or say a brief preliminary prayer. Orthodox Christians may kiss an icon. All of these small rituals, carried out by the individual, are an acknowledgment that one is entering a special place, and are part of the preparation for the sacred experience that is to come.

Once inside the church or temple, there may be further preliminaries to go through. Again, these may be practical, finding one's customary seat in a church or one's position, facing the mihrab or prayer niche, in a mosque. Or there may be more ritualistic preparations. An Orthodox Christian, for example, having made the sign of the cross and given a donation, will light a candle, thereby evoking one of the prime Christian symbols, light. Hindus also light candles. In addition, they ring a bell on entering the temple to tell God that they are there.

SACRED TEXT AND SACRED IMAGE

Forms of worship vary greatly from one religion to another, but there are common elements that recur in many faiths. All organized religions, for example, have sacred texts. A large part of religious ritual involves reading from or reciting such texts. The Bible of the Christians, the Jewish Torah, the Islamic Qur'an, Hindu writings such as the Upanishads and the Vedas, and Buddhist texts such as the Sutras, all play a vital part in religious rituals. Sometimes the book itself is a focus of the ceremony.

ISLAM
Mosques have a minaret, from which the *muezzin* can call the faithful to prayer. Inside the mosque, a niche called a mihrab indicates the direction of Mecca, towards which one must face during prayers.

FOCUSES FOR RITUAL

Religious buildings are designed specifically with ritual in mind. A mosque, therefore, has a large carpeted prayer-hall. A Christian church has rows of seats; the congregation usually sits and listens for some of the service. Most sacred buildings have a focus that often includes a vital symbol of the religion.

BUDDHISM
A statue of the Buddha often dominates Buddhist shrines. Buddha himself is not an object of worship, but Buddhists are expected to follow his teachings, and thereby hope to reach the state of nirvana, a freedom from attachment to life.

CHRISTIANITY
The focus of a Christian church is the high altar or Lord's table. It is here that the central ritual of the Eucharist is celebrated, at which Christians take bread and wine in remembrance of Christ's last meal with his disciples.

Judaism has absorbed sacred texts into its ritual perhaps more fully than any other religion. Worshippers are literally close to the text itself; men at prayer in the synagogue wear *tefillin*, small leather boxes containing sacred texts. These are joined to straps, by which they are attached to the arm and head. When reading the Hebrew scrolls of the Torah, the sacred text may not be touched – a silver reading finger may be used to follow the words. The scrolls themselves are wrapped in beautiful embroidered covers when not in use, just as in cultures where sacred texts appear in bound form, a rich leather, gilt or jewelled binding may be favoured.

In many religions, additional reminders of the sacred texts often appear on the walls of the temple or church. Thus mosques are embellished, not with images of the Prophet or great Muslims (Islam forbids figurative art), but with quotations from the Qur'an, in superb calligraphy. Most other religions look more indulgently on figurative art and use it to serve the sacred texts. Christian churches are often decorated with paintings, statues and stained-glass windows portraying Biblical subjects. Buddhist stupas may be adorned with carvings showing scenes from the life of the Buddha, and Hindu temples may contain carvings of episodes from the Ramayana and Mahabahrata, together with statues of the gods. All exist to direct the faithful to the content of the sacred text, to concentrate the mind on key elements of the faith, and often to provide a focus for prayer.

PRAYER

Why do people pray? First of all, humans are great communicators. Having conceived a faith in some sort of deity or supreme being, it is only natural that they should want to communicate with it. It can be no accident that many religions imagine their gods to have some human form. It might be an ancestor spirit (a former human), it might be a figure that looks like a person or has some human features, or it might be a god that spent some time on Earth in human form. All these manifestations of the deity hold out the possibility of communication with people, and of the building up of a relationship, and prayer provides the means by which that dialogue can take place.

In many religions, prayer is one of the observances that have to be followed correctly if one is to win a place in paradise, a fortunate reincarnation, and so on. In Islam, for example, observing the call to prayer is one of the five tenets or pillars of the religion. In most branches of Christianity prayer is expected, although prayers may be said in private as well as in formal church services.

The prayer itself can take many forms, from a short, repeated formula, to a long, improvised plea. But in most religions it is uttered in a set way, probably in a prescribed position. It is a highly ritualized, but also highly personal contact with the deity.

MUSIC

One way of emphasizing the importance of the sacred text is to set it to music. Music is one of the most common elements in all types of religious ceremony. It has different purposes in different religions, but in each case the effect is to heighten the impact of the ceremony, to achieve a more intense expression of faith than would have been possible with the words or actions alone.

Sometimes, the music underlines the words, helping to put across their message with both clarity and intensity. Nowhere is this clearer than with the Islamic call to prayer, sung by the muezzin, traditionally from the top of the mosque's minaret: 'God is most great. I testify that there is no God but Allah. I testify that Muhammad is God's Apostle. Come to prayer, come to security. God is most great.' It is an

entreaty of great power, rendered all the more compelling by being sung rather than shouted.

A similar blend of passion and clarity can also be heard in the chant of the Orthodox church and in the plainsong heard in Western Christian monasteries. But clarity sometimes loses out to musical expression. Church music of the Renaissance period, in which several parts harmonize with each other, produced music of stunning beauty, but frequently at the expense of the audibility of the words. So, too, did the custom of setting one syllable of a

word to many consecutive notes. It has been argued that this musical adornment was beautifying texts that everyone knew, so clarity was relatively unimportant. By contrast, in the Protestant churches, where music is widely used for hymns and sung services, the words can usually be clearly distinguished. Such music also makes it easier for the entire congregation to join in.

Hinduism has many uses for music, one of the best known of which is the chanting of the sacred syllable 'OM' or 'AUM'. The three

RITUAL AND ACTION

Many religious rituals are directly related to the world of human action. They may be designed to teach people the tenets of the religion, to show them how to behave, or how to perform religious acts correctly.

BUDDHISM

In some places it is traditional for Buddhists to free a caged bird at a shrine as a gesture of respect for the freedom of all living creatures.

ISLAM

Muslims learn the basic tenets of their religion and appropriate modes of behaviour by studying the Qur'an.

ROMAN CATHOLICISM

In the Catholic ritual of confession, the individual undertakes to do penance for past sins, one aim of which is to discourage such sin in the future.

sounds of which this syllable is made up recall Brahma (A), Vishnu (U) and Shiva (M). Thus the sound conjures up the core of Hinduism, while at the same time being perceived as the essence of all sounds.

Chants like these remind us that sacred music can exist without a written text. Indeed music was probably one of the earliest components of religious ceremony. Its power to affect the emotions, to calm the spirit or to whip it up into a frenzy of excitement, have been exploited by priests and shamans for thousands of years. In conjunction with dancing, it is widely used in animist religions to invoke the spirits and to create the right state of mind for the ceremony. From the Arctic shaman beating out a rhythm on his drum to the Australian Aborigine singing the story of his ancestry, music has played, and still plays, a crucial part in tribal religion.

RELIGIOUS PATHWAYS

Where there is a strong formal priestly hierarchy, as in many Christian churches, the procession provides an apt expression of religious principles. The senior clergyman is at the head, follwed by the lesser ranks in the hierarchy, who are in turn followed by lay members of the church. The procession thereby becomes an image of the structure of the church.

For Buddhists there is less of a hierarchy, but the procession still represents a key image of the religion. Both Christians and Buddhists, indeed, have a concept of a path which the individual should follow. For Christians it is a question of following Christ on the path to salvation. For Buddhists it is the eightfold path to enlightenment. Both paths are powerfully evoked by processions – both in public through the streets and within the church or monastery itself. Processions also form a useful method of 'advertisement' for religions looking for new recruits.

OFFERINGS AND SACRIFICES

Many religious ceremonies involve offerings. Pouring libations into the ground, to take the liquid towards the underworld, burning an offering so that its smoke ascends to the heavens, or just making a donation to the priest or shaman, all these are present in traditional religions. Modern organized religions also make use of offerings. Christians pass around a plate during services or pay money to light a candle and Hindus make offerings of flowers at the temple. Charity is one of the tenets of Islam, while donations to monks are expected in Buddhist societies. Offerings like these are a vital part of religious observance; they are also part of the wider human phenomenon of gift-giving, and so are also dealt with in the chapter of this book that deals with gifts.

Offerings, even the most straightforward monetary donations, are sacrifices. Christianity, a religion founded on the idea of sacrifice, has a unique way of remembering this. The Mass, Eucharist, or Lord's supper, re-enacts Christ's last supper with his disciples before he was taken from them. 'Do this in remembrance of me,' Christ said when breaking the bread. The mass thus remembers God's sacrifice of his only son for humanity's salvation. In partaking in this communion, Christians model themselves on Christ as they were told to do.

TEACHING

Religious education is a vital part of many faiths, and is frequently integrated into rituals. In traditional religions, it is often a question of teaching future initiates the ways of the shaman, usually in secret. But in the organized religions, teaching is frequently viewed as the means by which the tenets of the faith are passed on to all who will listen. The learning process is also fundamental to Judaism and

KRISHNA PROCESSION, USA
A movement with rituals based on Hinduism, the International Association for Krishna Consciousness (commonly known as the 'Hare Krishna' sect) was founded in 1965 in the United States. It is famous for its processions in which its followers walk through the streets chanting the mantra from which the movement gets its popular name.

DUSSHERA, INDIA
This Hindu festival is celebrated for ten days during the month of Asvina (September-October). There are processions in which images of the goddess Durga are taken through the streets. Plays based on episodes from the Ramayana epic are also performed.

RELIGIOUS PROCESSIONS

Wherever there are religions there are processions. These may celebrate festivals, they may follow a traditional pilgrimage route, or they may simply be a public expression the solidarity of the group. A procession, enhanced by special costumes, music, symbols, and even the display of holy relics, can act like an advertisement, encouraging bystanders to watch, cheer, give alms, or join in.

END OF RAMADAN, NIGERIA
The feast of Eid-ul-Fitr, marking the end of the fast of Ramadan, is celebrated throughout the Muslim world. For Muslims in Nigeria, for example, it is marked with processions and music in the streets.

CONTEMPLATION

Many religions have evolved special rituals to promote the attainment of a higher state of consciousness. Those who practise a 'soft' martial art like Tai Chi, who do yoga, or who tap gently on a drum or chant softly to themselves to induce a meditative state, are all using ritualistic behaviour in this way. Ritualized meditation may also be part of the daily timetable of the Christian monk, for example.

Islam. Jewish synagogues and Islamic mosques therefore incorporate schools in their buildings; and it was traditional for the Christian church to play an important part in the education of the young. For Buddhists, teaching is of central importance, since the very point of being a Buddhist is to learn how to follow the path toward enlightenment.

Sometimes religious teaching is fully integrated into the ritual, as in the sermon, which forms the heart of Christian (especially Protestant) services. Even where there is no such overt instruction, there are often readings from sacred texts. It is another example of the way communication is a key part of all religions.

In most religions, ritual plays a key part in this communication. It is true that there are some religions in which ritual plays a smaller part. Members of the Society of Friends or Quakers, for example, do not have formal religious services. Neither do they have clergy or churches. Instead they gather at Meeting Houses, where members may speak when 'the spirit moves them'. But religions like this are the exception rather than the rule. For most, ritual is an essential, and a fascinating, element.

RETREAT TO THE HILLS
Isolated hilltops – near to the heavens, away from human bustle and close to nature – are traditional places to meditate. Their awesome height and inhospitable terrain can seem to put human concerns in a different perspective. No wonder that for religious people from the Incas to the Buddhists, hills and mountains have had a special significance.

Art

Art is one of the most fundamental human activities. Both the 'high art' of painting and monumental sculpture and the more practical works of the applied artist go back to the beginnings of our time on Earth. Indeed, cave paintings, such as those at Lascaux, and numerous prehistoric carvings on stone and bone, are among the earliest traces of our early ancestors. Artistic expression has always been intimately connected with religion and ritual. Many scholars who have studied European Paleolithic cave art, for example, have suggested that these extraordinary works had religious origins. There are several possible reasons for this. The position of many of the paintings, in deep chambers that are virtually inaccessible, seems to support the view that the pictures were used to designate special sacred places. The arrangement of the painted images by which the rarest, or most terrifying, animal images appear in the innermost chambers seems to suggest some sort of hierarchy of the gods. Moreover, signs that some of the animal images have been marked as if by missiles suggests a pre-hunting ritual (see page 115). Other early works of art, from statuettes of generously proportioned women to stone circles, seem also to have religious origins.

The art of later times confirms the connection between art and religion. The great civilizations of Egypt, western Asia, China, Greece and Rome left behind rich artistic legacies. But it is the religous works of art, the temples and cult statues, the votive offerings and ritual objects, that are among the most memorable. This is also true in more recent, traditional societies, where artistic endeavour is often seen in masks or statues of gods or ancestors – religious objects that are deeply involved in ritual and custom.

ART AND THE SPIRIT
Celtic stone sculptures, prehistoric cave paintings, masks from Africa and South America, a votive figure from ancient Egypt, a ritual axe-head from China, and the stone circle at Stonehenge: works of art from all over the world and throughout history display the powerful connection between art and religion.

THE SUN AS SYMBOL
For thousands of years, both artists and priests have used the power of the sun as an image and symbol . The star that warms the Earth and ripens the crops also gives artists light by which to work. From the earliest times, people recognized the importance for our lives of its regular appearance and disappearance. Representations of the sun appear in the art of many different cultures - symbolizing power, life, creation, fertility and the changing seasons.

CAVE CRAFT
Palaeolithic cave paintings sometimes include stylized sun symbols. This example is from Las Batuecas, Spain.

ANCIENT EGYPT
For the Egyptians, the Sun God was perhaps the most important. Their 'wadjet eye' symbol represented the eye of the Sun God.

ANCIENT BABYLON
The god Shamash was the Babylonian sun deity. His symbol appears on seals, carved reliefs and boundary stones.

Non-visual art forms are still more closely connected with ritual. Dance and music are vital parts of religious rites from Christian ceremonies in Western Europe to fertility rites in southern Africa. Their use undoubtedly goes back to the earliest times.

Literature, too, is closely bound up in its origins with the religions and rituals of early civilizations. The lives and legends of the first gods gave rise to enduring myths. At first, no doubt, these myths were kept alive through the enactment of rituals and the telling of stories that were handed down orally, but as written cultures developed, these stories were written down. The earliest surviving narrative work, the Sumerian *Epic of Gilgamesh*, is an eloquent testimony to this myth-making.

The act of creation itself may be a deeply religious, or apparently magical process. This was probably the case with the cave paintings. Modern studies indicate that they were almost certainly created rapidly, and the speed with which images appeared would have been awe-inspiring to witnesses of their creation.

In some religions, especially the organized religions, which have substantial resources, many arts sometimes come together to make a large-scale spiritual statement. Architecture, painting, stained glass and sculpture in a medieval cathedral combined to create a fitting setting for worship. The ceremonies themselves would add further artistic expression – for example, in their use of music.

PREPARATION AND TRAINING

The power and importance of the work of art may be achieved through special preparation before the artist sets to work. For example, there was a tradition in the Melanesian islands of New Ireland in which special mortuary rites were held every few years to honour those who had died since the previous rites, and to honour the 'cosmic ancestors', the Sun and Moon. The ceremony would involve the production of a number of masks and sculptures, and the community would commission the best local artists to create

INDIA
This sun face appears on an 18th-century banner from Rajasthan, India.

AZTEC
The Aztecs worked out a calendar system that was represented on stones with this sun symbol.

SWITZERLAND
This sun mask is worn on St Martin's Day in Switzerland in a celebration of the passing of the seasons.

FRANCE
The light of the sun plays on the half-circle of a sundial supported by a stone angel on Chartres cathedral.

these. A special enclosure would be made and set aside in which the artists could work – they could not do the job in unsuitable conditions. The designs would be produced in close consultation with the village elders.

The importance of the ceremonies surrounding the making of these statues was such that each succeeding ceremony was expected to be more magnificent, and produce art that was more outstanding, than the previous one. This resulted in a highly elaborate artistic tradition, with a complex use of symbols that only the elders probably understood fully. Snake, bird and fish motifs were used separately, or in combination with each other, to produce carvings of fabulous creatures, while geometric patterns could be used to refer to the sun and moon or to local ancestors or heroes. And all these elements could intertwine within a single carving in a way that produced a unique effect.

The artist often has to undergo a highly structured training. Few western actors achieve success without submitting to the exacting

rituals of theatre school and showcase performances. The aspiring western classical musician, the young painter and the sculptor usually have similar formal apprenticeships, either in a school or with an individual teacher.

In other cultures the training may be still more structured. There is often a sense that there is no point trying to be an artist unless the rest of one's life is lived with absolute rectitude. In ancient China, for example, Confucius instructed his followers to develop their characters: 'Without character you will be unable to play on that instrument' Confucius said to a disciple who wanted to play the lute. The philosopher also acknowledged that art and ritual would give something back to the individual character.

Sometimes the interdependence of art and custom is taken still further, as in the case of the actors of traditional Japanese Kabuki theatre, who have to train for years and who must live an almost monastic life during this time. Similar steps are taken by many other artists who may undertake individual retreats

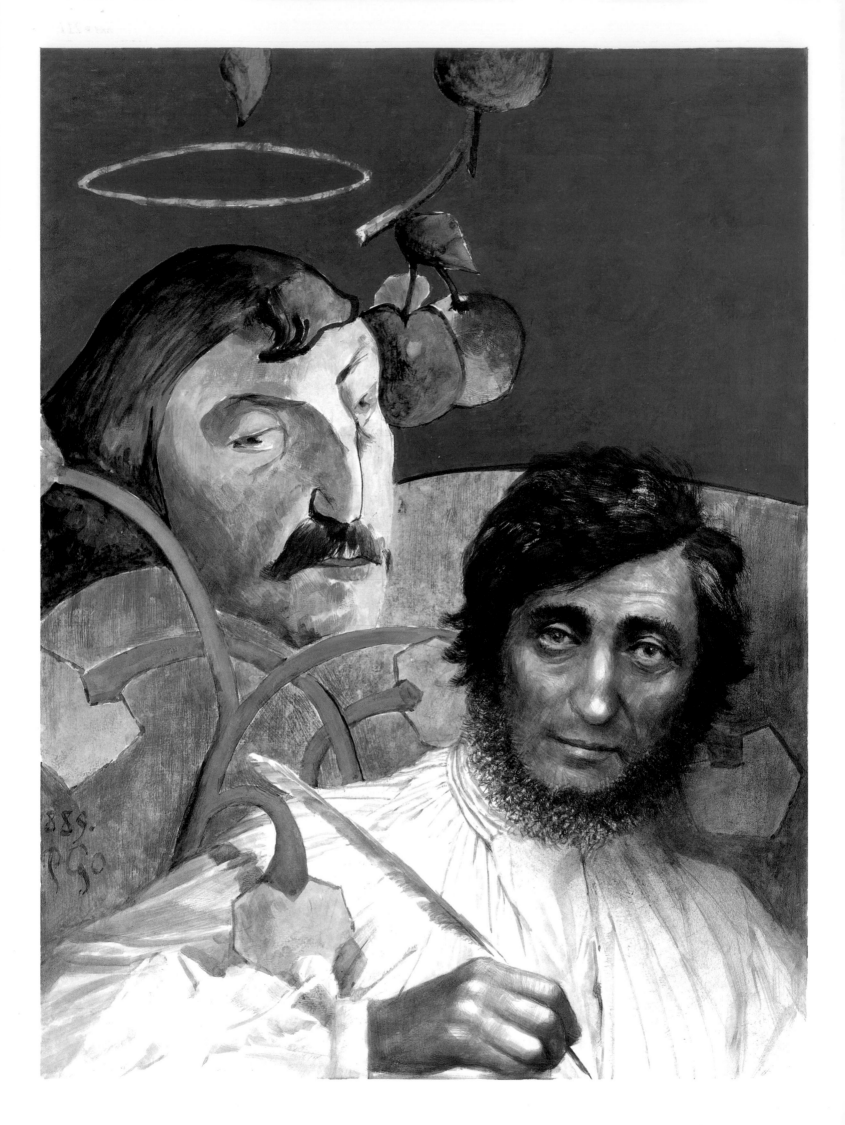

of different kinds. The 19th-century American writer Henry David Thoreau communing with nature, the French painter Paul Gaugin (1848-1903) abandoning Europe for the South Seas, and the modern British composer Sir Peter Maxwell Davies leaving the musical world of London for the isolation of Orkney – all in their different ways demonstrate aspects of the same need to escape from the familiar world in order to gain greater purity of artistic vision.

RITUALS BEFORE CREATION

Artists often describe the preparatory work they have to do before the actual act of creation as a ritual. It might be an actor applying make-up, a painter preparing a canvas, or even a photographer going through the motions of adjusting a large studio camera. Although they are basic practical necessities, these activities can be looked on as rituals. Artists evolve a specific routine, which they follow when they perform, that always has to be followed to ensure success.

CREATIVITY

French artist Paul Gaugin painted his *Self-portrait with Halo* in 1889, the year he decided to leave Europe for the South Pacific. By studying the art and lives of the people of Tahiti, and living among them, he was able to find new artistic inspiration. Henry David Thoreau was a 19th-century American writer who for two years lived a self-sufficient life in a hut on the edge of Walden Pond near Concord, Massachusetts. This very different retreat helped Thoreau in his work and gave him new artistic and philosophical insights.

There are also rituals or superstitions of less obvious usefulness that seem just as vital to those who observe them. The actor with 'lucky' personal possessions in the dressing room, the painter with the palette or work table arranged in a certain way, the writer who has to use a certain type of paper or notebook. Art – which often relies for its success on intangible qualities that some attribute to hard work, others to an almost supernatural inspiration – is perhaps more prone to such superstitions than any other human activity.

In some cases the artist may need to meditate or 'dream' before creating. As the contemporary Czech writer Bohumil Hrabal explained, 'I am always rushing around so that I can work two or three hours a day of inactive dreaming into my schedule.' This is the writer giving his mind a rest in the hope that the unconscious will take over, allowing different ideas to flow together and thereby enable him to come up with a new insight. Many artists have developed tricks to help them do this, many of which could be performed as rituals. The English poet A. E. Housman (1859 1936) would go for a two- or three-hour walk after lunch; the Russian writer Ivan Turgenev (1818-83) would immerse his feet in a bucket of hot water; and the German writer Friedrich Schiller (1759-1805) would inhale the smell of rotting apples.

THE POWER OF THE ARTIST

Artists are recognized in many societies as people with considerable personal power. In Polynesia, for example, an artist who was working on the carving of sacred images would be said to have a particular spiritual strength. His hands especially would be held to be full of power, so much so that it would be dangerous to touch them. Although such a view might seem far-fetched to someone outside this society, one only has to consider the degree of involvement and concentration that most artists give to their work to understand the idea that there is some sort of hidden power behind the act of creation.

In many cultures, the artist works alone, although the works he or she creates may be the cause of communal feasting and celebration. In the Pacific islands of the New Hebrides, for example, one of the most important ritual objects is the drum or slit gong. These often beautifully decorated objects are used to accompany various dances. When a man commissions a new slit gong he also gives a feast when the finished instrument is set up on the dancing ground. There are obvious parallels in western art, where opening nights of exhibitions are marked with a private view at which celebration and socializing are at least as important as looking at the art.

Sometimes the celebrations surrounding the creation of a new work are more elaborate than this. One of the most notable examples was a ceremony that used to be held on the coasts of southern Papua New Guinea. The ceremony normally took place when a series of misfortunes had befallen the people – perhaps several consecutive crop failures or a higher-than-normal number of deaths. First, a special mask house would be built; this in itself was a major project, since the structure would be based on a heavy framework of logs and would have a large thatched roof. Then the men of each clan would gather in the house and make and paint tall oval masks. Each clan would create a mask that would represent a particular benefactor spirit. All the masks would have different designs, but they would all be in the same style, decorated with abstract and stylized facial patterns in pastel shades on a grey background. The work of creation would last a long time, sometimes months, occasionally even years. Finally, each mask would be donned by a man, and the members of his clan would gather around the mask and process along the coast of the island. This period of jubilation would culminate in a

THE ART OF THE MASK HOUSE

In many societies, the art that is required for ritual has to be made according to strict rules. In Melanesia and New Guinea, the lavishly decorated ceremonial masks had to be made in a building erected specially for this purpose. The large size of the mask house, and the amount of time spent building it are testimony to the importance of the masks in the ceremonies for which

feast. There might also be initiation ceremonies for the youth of the clan. Then the masks would be taken to a special courtyard and ceremonially thanked for their participation in the festival before being destroyed by fire.

This ceremony was intended to foster the health and good fortune of the people by banishing disease and promoting a good

they were designed. The men would gather in the mask house to make masks representing different ancestor spirits. The impact of the completed masks was enhanced by the secrecy surrounding their creation and the spectacle of their revelation in a procession along the coast.

harvest; it allowed the young people to be initiated; it enabled the elders to maintain their all-important contact with the world of the spirits; and it gave the mask-makers a vital outlet for their skills. Only the elders knew the full significance of the designs on the masks, but all were affected by their power, which was so great that the masks had to be destroyed at the end of the ritual. There are few stronger examples of the spritual power of art over an entire society.

BECOMING A SPIRIT

Many works of art , particularly in traditional societies, are so powerful that they are perceived in some way to become what they represent. The Papuan masks are not mere representations of the spirits: when worn by the appropriate clan members they *are* the spirits. In many societies that use masks, the altered state that people can enter when they are engaged in artistic creation or performance, combined with the heightened spiritual awareness of a religious ceremony, creates an identification between mask, spirit and wearer. This is an effect that is visible all over the

PAPUA NEW GUINEA
This tamato (spirit) mask is made of clay.

world. The native Pueblo peoples of the southwestern United States, for example, use masks to impersonate and 'become' the revered *kachina* spirits. These spirits are gods of fertility and well-being. Their cult is centred on circular chambers called *kivas*, and the spirits, in the form of masked cult members, come to earth from time to time, arriving from the underworld by way of the *kivas* to take part in sacred ceremonies. While these are going on, the cult member is identified with the *kachina* spirit.

Pueblo men also carve small wooden dolls that represent the *kachina* spirits. These are made according to strict rules: the spirit must be portrayed correctly in every detail, including its clothing and mask. Part of the ceremony in which the masked dancers take

PUEBLO PEOPLE
On this *kachina* figure, the eyes are shown as rain clouds and the eyelashes as rain.

part involves giving these dolls to the children, who take them and display them prominently in their homes. The idea is that each household should always be in the presence of the spirit.

In a similar way, the spiritual power of art can also be felt when people carry art objects as some form of badge of belonging. This is a widespread practice. For example, the Bapende people of the western Congo traditionally wear a miniature ivory mask on a cord around their necks. This indicates membership of a secret society. Another Congo people, the

NIGERIA
This mask was worn by members of the secret society of the Igbo people.

Warenga, use small masks in a similar way, with different designs representing the grades attained by the wearer in the secret society. Clearly the art object is operating here much more like a symbol. But even here, by recalling larger ceremonial masks, the badge of belonging has a certain spiritual power. In a similar way, the wearing of military medals or other awards sometimes evokes respect in western societies.

Another use of the spiritual power of art is

NEW ZEALAND
This wood carving represents the Maori god Tangaroa. The god was said to enter the wood and speak through the voice of the priest.

found in another Melanesian culture, on the island of Malekula. Here the people believe that it is necessary gradually to accrue spiritual power throughout one's life; without this power it is not possible to have life after death. To acquire spiritual power, the individual has to pass through a series of social grades, each of which would be marked by the right to prepare a certain type of carving and to use such a carving in rituals. The carving would represent an ancestor who had attained the social grade to which the person aspired. It might also represent more universal symbols, such as the hawk and the sun, both emblems of an early ancestor who was said to have brought the wild boar, a sacred animal, to the island. Carvings representing an ancestor of a particular grade could only be used once:

another carving would be required when one rose to the next social grade.

CEREMONY AND PERFORMANCE

The visual arts, theatre, and religion are often bound closely together in sacred ceremony. Nowhere is this clearer than in a ritual performed by the Duwamish people of the northwestern American coast. One of the beliefs of these people was that a person's soul could go temporarily missing. A symbolic journey would be enacted to search for and recover the soul from the spirits of the dead. A group of shamans and other people would usually come together for such a ceremony. The shamans would have a carving representing a spirit and a number of painted ceremonial boards. The first stage of the ritual was to repaint the designs on the ceremonial boards. Then the boards and figures were set up indoors in the shape of the outline of a canoe. The shamans and the other participants would then enact the journey in the 'canoe', until they arrived in the spirit world, where they would search for the lost soul. After a ritual fight with the spirits they returned in their 'canoe' to the land of the living and restored the soul to its rightful owner. In this ceremony, a mixture of religious, social, therapeutic ends were served, all of which would have been impossible without the central artistic activities of the painting and the re-enactment.

Sometimes a sacred performance takes place regularly. In medieval Europe the craft guilds in some towns got together annually to produce spectacular religious dramas, the miracle or mystery plays. An entire cycle of plays would enact the major stories from the Bible, from the creation to Christ's resurrection and beyond, often at considerable expense. Performances like this represented a coming together of the community, uniting disparate social groups and confirming the

PERFORMANCE AND RITUAL

Traditional forms of theatre, such as mime, pantomime and animal dances are closely related to the world of ritual. They often re-enact ancient myths and legends, like the Chinese lion dance or the European mystery play, and they often use traditional masks, as in the Italian *commedia dell'arte*. Their use of archetypal images and timeless symbols links them more closely than any other type of performance to the displays of the shaman and the priest.

central power of the crafts guilds.

A well-known example of the use of mystery plays as a form of communal artistic expression can still be seen in Oberammergau in the Bavarian alps. In 1633 the villagers were miraculously saved from the plague. As a result, the community vowed to perform a lengthy passion play every ten years, in thanks for their deliverance.

Organized religion benefits greatly from performances like these: they spread the tenets of the religion in an accessible and popular way. What is more, the collaboration and effort needed to stage such complex productions also binds societies and gives people kinds of fulfilment that they might not otherwise know. Such benefits are seen in many cultures: the dances of lion and dragon seen in Chinese street celebrations at New Year and on other occasions; the masked cavortings of Venetian and South American carnivals; the great community performances of episodes from the Hindu myths in English cities such as Leicester; the work of radical theatre companies involving whole communities in their work; even the small amateur theatre group in a village hall – all these activities use the almost magical, celebratory power of art to bring groups of people closer together.

All the collective arts, those that need a group of people in order to make them happen, can work in this way. And if we rarely nowadays have annual cycles of mystery plays performed in our cities, we often have annual arts festivals, where the special qualities of the arts, especially the performing arts, are celebrated.

Symbolic images

Perhaps the most significant aspect of art in its relation to ritual is the ability of the artist to create symbolic images that can stand for gods, ancestors or any other being at the focus of a ceremony, and to which sometimes are ascribed supernatural powers. A notable example of this in the Christian West is the icon. Icons are usually portraits of saints or of Christ. Orthodox Christians set them up both in churches and in homes. They become focuses for devotion: candles are lit in front of them, incense is burned, prayers are said.

The power of icons is such that there are many traditions of miracles associated with them: icons are said to speak or to weep; prayers said to them are held to bring about miracles; they may bleed if stabbed by an unbeliever; eating a fragment of paint or plaster from an icon may cure a disease; and even carrying an icon may bring good fortune – soldiers used to take them into battle.

There are similar traditions of weeping statues and images that apparently have healing power in the Roman Catholic church. In both traditions the work of art is more than a mere representation of a saint or of God. They are held to partake in some way of the essence of the deity.

Islamic tradition generally forbids representative art. To attempt to imitate the creator by painting portraits is a kind of blasphemy. But the intricate patterns and elegant designs of Islamic art often have their own spiritual meanings. Gardens, like those at the Taj Mahal and the Alhambra, were conceived as images of paradise. Such gardens are often divided into four squares – four was the holiest of numbers – containing cypress trees, symbolizing death, and fruit trees, symbolizing life.

In Japanese Zen Buddhism, gardens are made to symbolize the whole of creation. They therefore include sand, which stands for water, and rocks, which represent mountains. Above all, Zen gardens evoke an atmosphere of calm, creating an ideal setting for contemplation.

Even the smaller-scale creations of the religious artist, such as statuettes of the deity, often take on a sort of 'spiritual essence' for the believer. A similar power can be attached to

symbols with meanings that are buried even deeper. One motif that has special meanings is the maze or labyrinth. It is a good example of the way in which an artistic image can carry more than one meaning. Labyrinths go back thousands of years, at least to the Cretan legend of the minotaur, the half-bull, half-human beast, that King Minos is supposed to have kept at the heart of a labyrinth and that Theseus is said to have slain. This legend evokes a labyrinth which is confusing, dark and dangerous. But there is also the later, Christian idea of the labyrinth, in which the one correct path to the centre symbolizes the righteous path of the believer. So, Christian cathedral builders and more recent garden designers have included mazes in their creations. Even today, people cannot resist 'treading the labyrinth' – walking the route to the centre or exit – although few of them will realize that they are re-enacting a symbolic Christian pilgrimage or the route of the anxious Theseus on his way to slay the beast.

What is striking about such symbolic images, then, is that they communicate something of their meaning even to people from distant cultures. One does not have to be a Muslim to appreciate the heavenly proportions of the gardens at the Taj Mahal; non-Christians can perceive the beauty of an icon, and even respect some of the reverence accorded these images; men and women from the West can look at a mask from Africa and be moved by its power. Art and its rituals, like the other ceremonies described in this book, triumphantly cross cultures and frontiers, bringing us closer together.

LOOKING TOWARDS ANOTHER WORLD
The Taj Mahal, with its gardens laid out as an Islamic symbol of paradise; an African mask showing the face of a spirit; a labyrinth, indicating the one way towards God; an icon portraying a Christian saint: all these examples illustrate the ability of art to lead us into other worlds, to give us visions of existence that stretch beyond the everyday. Whatever our faith and our culture, both art and ritual have the ability to uplift us.

Index

References to illustrations are shown in italics